The Lucky Few

Elwood Carlson

The Lucky Few

Between the Greatest Generation and the Baby Boom

 Springer

Elwood Carlson
Florida State University
Center for Demography and
Population Health
Tallahassee FL 32306
USA
ecarlson@fsu.edu

Cover: Original cover illustration by Pete Escobedo, www.EscoArts.com

ISBN (HB): 978-1-4020-8540-6   e-ISBN: 978-1-4020-8541-3
ISBN (PB): 978-1-4020-8850-6

Library of Congress Control Number: 2008927893

Contents

List of Figures

Preface

The idea for this book arose out of a collision of theoretical writings with empirical data, as so often is the case in demographic research. The theoretical ideas began to bubble and ferment many years ago, after adopting Richard Easterlin's marvelous book, *Birth and Fortune*, for an undergraduate population course and re-reading his arguments about generation size carefully. Demographers are never far from ideas about cohort phenomena, though, and encounters with the writings of Norman Ryder as well as conversations with Tomas Frejka and other cohort-oriented scholars enriched the stew of ideas.

The empirical data that collided with these ideas first came to my attention as a member of NIH review study sections, where I first learned in excruciating detail about the huge IPUMS project at Minnesota that eventually mined public use microdata samples out of more than a century of manuscript censuses, and later out of all the available Current Population Surveys as well. Even at the time, I recall thinking what a marvelous resource these PUMS data would be, and resolved to use them in my own research one day.

With the completion of *The Lucky Few*, that day would appear to have arrived. After toying with these ideas, sporadically at first but more and more intensively for roughly a decade, the past couple of years have finally yielded up the entire project. Specialized scholars in countless fields will find objectionable superficiality and over-generalizations in every section of every chapter, but my intent has been to touch on as many aspects of this remarkable generation's life course as possible, and to compare them to all the other generations living through the 20th century. Such a wide-angle goal demands that many related issues arising out of every topic, and many nuances of theory and intricate details of previous research, must be ignored or glossed over in order to crowd the whole tapestry of this generational perspective into a single, digestible volume. If readers find lacunae in the discussion or otherwise take issue with the presentation, my fondest hope is that they may be stimulated to extend and refine the ideas in question, advancing our understanding in the process.

In expressing my thanks for help with the book, first place must go to Charles B. Nam. Not only was he the first person to read the earliest, crudest drafts of the manuscript and provide countless good ideas, references and commentary, but the Charles B. Nam Professorship that he helped to establish at Florida State University has allowed me the flexibility of time and resources needed to hammer out the manuscript while also maintaining a career of teaching, other research, and university service. Peter Morrison's enthusiasm about the project helped me move it to the "front burner" and complete the task after years of less-intense efforts, and his detailed editorial commentary on every chapter helped to bring the text up at least part-way toward the attention-grabbing clarity of his own writing. Similar encouragement and editorial suggestions from Dudley Poston also helped to move the manuscript forward and to improve the final draft. The entire undertaking would have been impossible without the publicly-available IPUMS data sets compiled and maintained on the internet by the University of Minnesota, and library staff at FSU's Strozier library helped me several times to locate both archived data in print format, and important references for the text. I am grateful to the Department of Sociology and Florida State University for financial support of professional illustrations for the book cover.

My largest single debt of gratitude, however, goes to the clever blue-eyed economist in my life, my wife Judy, who carefully and critically read every page and inspected every figure in the manuscript. Her thoughtful, often insightful questions and corrections led me to countless improvements of the manuscript, sometimes small but sometimes very large and substantively critical to the overall argument. I have no illusions that every reader will approach *The Lucky Few* with the same intensity and care that she did, but I am much happier and more confident about the manuscript after incorporating her suggestions.

Finally, I dedicate *The Lucky Few* to the members of every American generation of the twentieth century, especially to the Lucky Few themselves, but also to my Generation X daughters Lisa and Ingrid, in the hopes that their small generation eventually may experience some of the remarkable good fortune that has followed the Lucky Few through most of their lives.

Tallahassee, Florida   Elwood Carlson
February 2008

Introduction

Individual effort is one factor affecting a person's destiny. But forces beyond the control of the individual also play a role in determining one's life, and for the bulk of the population they may often play a crucial role. In this volume, Woody Carlson argues that Americans fortunate enough to be born between 1929 and 1945 – "the Lucky Few" – achieved success and self-fulfillment to an extent much greater than that of prior or succeeding generations, and that the exceptional situation of the Lucky Few was largely because of a fortuitous conjuncture of historical circumstances.

In Carlson's view the principal reason for the Lucky Few's success was being born in a period when birth rates were exceptionally low, and thus being a generation of unusually small numbers – hence the "Few" of the book's title. Small numbers mean, among other things, more parental attention to children; smaller class size at school and greater opportunities for extracurricular prominence – making the team, being selected for a leading acting role, becoming editor of the school paper, being elected class officer, and so on. Smaller numbers mean also, on reaching adulthood, greater opportunities for jobs and promotion. Small numbers, however, do not in themselves guarantee exceptional outcomes, and, as Carlson points out, the Lucky Few, on reaching the labor market, were also the beneficiaries of an exceptionally long post World-War II economic boom, and absence of significant competition from immigrants.

This is not an impressionistic argument based on a few personal interviews with individuals chosen to illustrate the author's thesis. Carlson makes his case quantitatively, with representative portrayals of successive generations that encompass demographic, economic, social, and political circumstances. His interest is in the everyday life of the great mass of people in each generation. His primary data are the invaluable micro-data computer files constructed in recent decades from the manuscript Censuses of Population and Housing. Based on these data, he does numerous original calculations to compare the state of seven generations spanning the twentieth century. These analyses are supplemented by sample survey data from multiple sources. All of this skillful and painstaking work is distilled into some 50 or more charts that are the skeleton that provides the framework on which this broad social history is hung.

Carlson's seven generations range from those he calls "New Worlders", born 1871–1889, to "New Boomers", born 1983 through 2001 – the latter only starting to reach adulthood now. The identification of these generations is based upon distinctive historical epochs and events that shaped the lives of each – war, economic depression, low fertility, immigration, and the like. As Carlson himself would doubtless admit, the precise dating of generational boundaries is somewhat arbitrary – for example, is the average experience of the "Good Warriors" born in 1927 or 1928 very much different from the "Lucky Few" born 1929 or 1930? But the generations he identifies seem, by and large, plausible. Moreover, the cohort comparisons presented in the graphs and the accompanying text discussion contribute much more than delimiting the distinctive features of the Lucky Few. They bring out also, for example, long term trends in such things as occupational structure and mortality, and enable us to see the circumstances of recently born generations, such as "Gen-X'ers" in the perspective of their predecessors. Typically, Carlson makes such cross-generational comparisons at the same life cycle stage to avoid the confounding effects of age.

Carlson – himself a member of the Baby Boom generation – is a highly respected demographer and sociologist. An economist might have liked to see more on the material circumstances of the various generations, such as their income history and occupational mobility, to the extent made possible by the data available. Also, in discussing the comparative fortunes of the latest "small numbers" cohort, Generation X (born 1965–1982), attention might have been paid to the impact on their economic circumstances of the labor market hangover from the exceptionally large predecessor Baby Boom cohort, the "saturation effect", so aptly identified in Diane Macunovich's *Birth Quake* (University of Chicago Press, 2002). But it is in the nature of scholarship never to be satisfied – the great volume of Carlson's work and findings inevitably whets one's appetite for more.

I have touched on the "Few" in the volume's title, but what of the "Lucky"? Carlson does not really say in so many words in what way the "Lucky" Few were particularly fortunate. He mentions and provides some evidence of the exceptional labor market experiences of both men and women in that generation. Yet, on a per household member basis, it is almost certainly the case that at the same life cycle stage, the absolute real income of generations subsequent to the Lucky Few was greater. Also, more recent generations have probably benefited at least as much as the Lucky Few from the continuous influx of new consumer goods. True, the job market for men has deteriorated, but that for women had gotten better with the shattering of the Glass Ceiling. Moreover, the latest generations are better educated than the Lucky Few and have longer life expectancy.

In short, on several important objective indicators – income, education, life expectancy – the Lucky Few were not clearly better off than their successors. What is truly distinctive about the Lucky Few in the analysis presented here is their family circumstances. As Carlson demonstrates, both as children and parents the Lucky Few lived much more than other twentieth-century generations in nuclear households. They married younger, had more children, and mothers stayed at home while raising the children, deferring labor force re-entry to later ages. The Lucky Few generation was the last, and perhaps fullest, exemplar of the traditional family. Carlson clearly views these family circumstances as desirable – he mentions, for example, that Gen X was not saved from the "general deterioration of the family as a care-giving institution". He recognizes, however, that this judgment might not warrant the characterization "lucky" by those of a feminist disposition.

I tend to agree, however, that the Lucky Few were lucky, though for a somewhat different reason. The missing ingredient in the story is, in my view, the material aspirations of each generation – a factor not easily quantified and well beyond the purview of government statisticians. Ordinarily, material aspirations increase from one generation to the next as the onward march of economic growth assures that each successive generation is raised in conditions of greater affluence and thereby acquires higher material standards of the good life. The Lucky Few were the exception to this long term trend. They were born precisely in the period of major economic deprivation for consumers – the Great Depression and World War II. As a result the material circumstances of the households in which they were raised, and, consequently, their material aspirations, failed to follow the normal upward trend. But their ability to realize their aspirations was exceptional, thanks, as Carlson point out, to an extraordinary growth of labor demand coupled with unusually short labor supply. It is this combination of disproportionately low material aspirations and unusually high realized income that accounts for their exceptional demographic behavior in family forming years and their early retirement from the labor market later in life. Compared with other generations the Lucky Few may not have been so exceptional in terms of objective indicators, but relative to their aspirations, they did indeed achieve greater success and self-fulfillment. Thus, Carlson is right, I believe, in identifying the generation as the "Lucky Few", and in telling succinctly so much of its story here.

Pasadena, California   Richard A. Easterlin
January 2008

Chapter 1
Who are the Lucky Few?

Contents

Faces of the Lucky Few

Twelve astronauts have walked on the surface of the Moon. Eleven of those twelve (including Neil Armstrong, the first man on the Moon) belonged to the Lucky Few, a special group of Americans who form the subject of this book. NASA's Apollo program actually launched fourteen astronauts for lunar landings, but the crew of Apollo 13 had to abort their mission when they barely survived a disaster in space. Apollo flights 11–17 each flew from the Earth with a crew of three. The command module pilot stayed in orbit while the other two astronauts landed on the Moon. In all, 19 of the 21 Apollo astronauts flying these seven lunar landing missions were members of the Lucky Few, with only Commanders Jim Lovell of Apollo 13 and Al Shepard of Apollo 14 as outsiders.

In addition to eleven of the twelve Moon-walkers, astronomers Carl Sagan (who spent his share of time looking at the Moon) and Joseph H. Taylor (winner of a Nobel Prize for discovery of the first pulsar) also belong to this selective group. However, the Lucky Few is not a scientific association. Members come from all walks of life, including immigrants from other countries who have had a major impact on life in the United States. These opening pages attempt to convey a sense of both their diversity and their accomplishments.

The Lucky Few in Public Life

As the Civil Rights movement swept across the United States in the second half of the twentieth century, the Reverend Martin Luther King Jr. left his pulpit to lead the way toward his dream for America. Dr. King was a member of the Lucky Few. So was James Meredith, who after his tour of duty in the U.S. Air Force returned to Mississippi to enroll (over fierce local protests, and with the help of National Guard troops) in the University of Mississippi as its first black student. Gloria Steinem, feminist pioneer and founder of MS. magazine, belongs to the Lucky Few.

When the United States launched operation Desert Storm to wrest Kuwait from the forces of Saddam Hussein in the early 1990s, Lucky Few Generals Norman Schwartzkopf and Colin Powell led their forces to swift victory across the deserts of the Middle East while Lucky Few General Wesley Clark coordinated the domination of the skies above them.

The first Hispanic Surgeon General of the United States and also the first woman to hold the job, Antonia Novello, is a member of the Lucky Few. So is Jocelyn Elders, the first black woman appointed to the same position. Both of the first female Justices on the United States Supreme Court, Sandra Day O'Connor and Ruth Bader Ginsberg, belong to the Lucky Few. In fact, for a time they joined with Justices Stephen E. Breyer, Anthony M. Kennedy, Antonin Scalia and David H. Souter to yield a Lucky Few two-thirds majority on the High Court.

The Lucky Few also includes many high-level elected officials. Some notable examples include Arizona Senator John McCain, California Senator Dianne Feinstein, Colorado Senators Ben Nighthorse Campbell and Gary Hart, Connecticut Senator Joseph Lieberman, Georgia Senator Zell Miller, Illinois Senator Carol Mosley Braun and Congressman and Cabinet Officer Donald Rumsfeld,

Missouri Senator and Cabinet Officer John Ashcroft, New York Governor Mario Cuomo and Congressman Jack Kemp, Pennsylvania Senator Henry Heinz, Rhode Island Governor Pierre DuPont, Texas Governor Ann Richards and Senator Kay Bailey Hutchinson, and Wyoming Congressman and Vice President Dick Cheney. Many other names could be added to this political list, but even at its most complete it would be as notable for the many famous missing names as for those included. In fact, at this writing no President of the United States has ever been a member of the Lucky Few.

The Lucky Few in Business

Where the Lucky Few *really* shines, however, is in the world of business and finance. If, in the words of President Calvin Coolidge, "the business of America is business," this has been doubly true for the Lucky Few. Although this theme furnishes one focus for later chapters of the book, even an introduction to the Lucky Few would be impossible without at least a little attention to this side of the picture. Some of the richest people in the world, including investment tycoon Warren Buffett and media mogul Ted Turner, all belong to the Lucky Few. Liz Claiborne created a cosmetics and fashion empire whose impact reaches throughout our society. Calvin Klein began his business empire with jeans and underwear, but has diversified in countless directions. Michael Eisner built a successful media career with the Walt Disney Company. Jack Welch became legendary as the ruthless CEO of the General Electric Corporation. All belong to the Lucky Few. On the other hand, Donald Trump, Lee Iacocca and Bill Gates just missed being members and will never be allowed to join.

Many members of the Lucky Few may not be household names, but the results of their business achievements are familiar to most Americans. John C. Bogle (born in Montclair, New Jersey in 1929) was hired by Wellington Management Company founder Walter Morgan immediately after graduating from Princeton in 1951. After working in the investment business for 23 years, in 1974 Bogle in his turn founded Vanguard, one of the largest and most successful investment firms in America. Self-educated Dee Ward Hock (born in Utah in 1929) became CEO of the newly formed National Bank-Americard Corporation in 1970, which he renamed Visa International in 1977.

Hock led the way into the modern era of electronic bank transfers, magnetic strips on credit cards, and the internationalization of financial services. Phillip H. Knight (born in 1938) excelled as a track star under legendary coach Bill Bowerman at the University of Oregon while studying accounting. His Nike sports shoe company has made him one of the 30 richest men in America. Thomas B. Monaghan (born in Michigan in 1937) bought a small pizza shop in Ypsilanti named Dominick's, renamed it Domino's Pizza, and over the next four decades built one of the largest restaurant conglomerates in the country. Whitney MacMillan, a direct descendant of founder William Cargill, made his fortune as the last family CEO of the family-owned Cargill Incorporated, the unquestioned king of America's agribusiness sector. John S. Reed, as the CEO of Citicorp, helped to pioneer the introduction of ATM machines in banks and other businesses.

Although many of these successful business leaders consciously avoid the public spotlight, others have found a place in that spotlight – sometimes by choice, and sometimes involuntarily. One-time IBM salesman, EDS founder and presidential candidate H. Ross Perot made the transition from business to public life by choice. On the other hand, Martha Stewart and Ivan Boesky both worked hard to become rich and successful. Both made mistakes and went to jail in the glare of media spotlights. Both are members of the Lucky Few. Kenneth Lay, the Enron CEO whose greed and arrogance inflicted incredible damage on the U.S. economy, belonged to the Lucky Few.

The Lucky Few in Sports

In the first Super Bowl football game ever played in January 1967, both starting quarterback Bart Starr of the Green Bay Packers and starting quarterback Len Dawson of the Kansas City Chiefs were members of the Lucky Few, like other football stars including Jim Brown, Dick Butkus, Frank Gifford, Joe Namath, Gayle Sayers, Johnny Unitas, and many others.

Although some baseball greats such as Ted Williams, Reggie Jackson or Mark McGwire will never be admitted to the ranks of Lucky Few, the world of professional baseball is even better-represented than professional football. Lucky Few baseball legends include players like Hank Aaron, Howard "Mickey" Mantle and Willie

Mays, along with a long list of their contemporaries. Even Pete Rose, whose baseball claim to fame is somewhat different, can be counted among the Lucky Few.

Likewise, famed golfers such as Jack Niklaus, Arnold Palmer, Lee Trevino and Kathy Whitworth belong to the Lucky few. On the other hand, Nancy Lopez and Tiger Woods can never join. Boxing legends Joe Frazier and Mohammed Ali are part of the Lucky Few, but George Foreman and Mike Tyson are not. Virgil Runnels (better known to wrestling fans as Dusty Rhodes) belongs to the Lucky Few, but neither Hulk Hogan (who went on to star in movies) nor Jesse Ventura (who went on to be Governor of Minnesota) are members. One of the greatest jockeys of all time, Willie Shoemaker, was a member of the Lucky Few.

The Lucky Few in Music

In the world of music, U.S.-born conductors James Levine and Leonard Slatkin join immigrants such as Zubin Mehta from India, Lorin Maazel from France, Seiji Ozawa from Japan or Andre Previn from Germany, who all qualify for Lucky Few membership.

In almost every branch of modern popular music, members of the Lucky Few appear as founding artists. The quintessential American pop music icon of the twentieth century, Elvis Presley, belonged to the Lucky Few. If they had become Americans, every one of the Beatles (plus Eric Clapton, Mick Jagger, Keith Richards and others) would count among the Lucky Few. As it is, rock music legends from Roberta Flack, Grace Slick and Janis Joplin to Jimi Hendrix, Jim Morrison and Van Morrison all come from the ranks of the Lucky Few. Their progress was charted for many years on American Bandstand by another Lucky Few member, the "eternal teenager," Dick Clark.

Country music practically owes its foundations to the Lucky Few. Johnny Cash, Waylon Jennings, Merle Haggard, Willie Nelson, Kenny Rogers, Tammy Wynette, and Charley Pride only begin to give an idea about how much the Lucky Few have shaped this musical tradition.

In every branch of music, though, a few of the most outstanding contributors will never have a chance to join the Lucky Few. Hank Williams fits that mold for country music. Bruce Springsteen is left out when it comes to rock and roll, as is James Brown when we consider the blues or soul. On the other hand, the Lucky Few do count among their number people such as Ray Charles, Aretha Franklin, Gladys Knight, Curtis Mayfield, Little Richard, Diana Ross and Barry White.

The Lucky Few also created an entire new era for folk music in the United States through songs of members like Bob Dylan, Paul Simon and Art Garfunkel, and an impressive contingent of women including Joan Baez, Carole King, Joni Mitchell and Carly Simon. Other Lucky Few musicians include Burt Bacharach, Neil Diamond, Robert Goulet, Tom Jones, Bob Marley, Ricky Nelson, Barbra Streisand, and Neil Young.

The Lucky Few in Television and Movies

The Lucky Few often appeared on television, including news anchormen Dan Rather, Tom Brokaw or Jim Lehrer, investigative reporters from the ridiculous (Geraldo Rivera) to the sublime (Barbara Walters), sports commentator John Madden, journalists Bill Moyers and Tony Brown, comedienne Carol Burnett, comedian Bill Cosby, and commentator Regis Philbin. In keeping with the pattern already emerging, of course, some well-known television personalities such as Jay Leno, David Letterman and Oprah Winfrey (as well as the late and lamented Fred Rogers of Mr. Rogers' Neighborhood and Bob Keeshan, better known as Captain Kangaroo) have been excluded from the Lucky Few.

Putting images on the Silver Screen also has been an occupation for Lucky Few movie directors Francis Ford Coppola, George Lucas and Martin Scorsese, but director Steven Speilberg will never gain admission to the selective group. Hollywood has conferred fame and fortune on Lucky Few actors Woody Allen, Julie Andrews, Robert DeNiro, Danny DeVito, Clint Eastwood, Barbara Eden, brother and sister Jane and Peter Fonda (but not their father Henry), Harrison Ford, Goldie Hawn, Dennis Hopper, Steve Martin, Bette Midler, Mary Tylor Moore, Jack Nicholson, Leonard Nimoy, Al Pacino, Richard Pryor, Robert Redford, Elizabeth Taylor (but not her former husband Richard Burton), Raquel Welch, and Gene Wilder. A full list could go on literally for pages. Again, though, in addition to a few names noted above, other equally famous stars find themselves excluded from membership. Marlon Brando, James Garner, Mel Gibson, Tom Hanks, Jerry Lewis, Marilyn Monroe and Paul Newman can never aspire to be part of the Lucky Few.

Membership in the Lucky Few

In case anyone might be interested in joining the mysterious Lucky Few, the bad news is that the membership list was closed long ago, at the end of 1945. No new members have been accepted since that time. There has never been any actual application process for membership. Virtually none of the members of the Lucky Few even have been aware that they belong to the group. This is so because membership in the Lucky Few is defined simply by the year you were born. Everyone in the United States born from 1929 to 1945 is automatically a member, and nobody else is allowed in the group. The Lucky Few, in other words, is what is familiarly known as a generation.

Defining Generations

So what is a generation? The demographic definition of a generation is very precise: simply observe the age of a parent at a baby's birth. The years between births of parent and child give the length of the generation. In their classic study of generations in history, William Strauss and Neil Howe (1991) call this feature of kinship the family generation. We can find the length of a generation easily for any individual – my mother had reached age 38 when I was born, but family generations may be only half that long. Ryder (1965) reserved the term generation for such units of kinship structure rather than for groups of people within a broad age span (say, childhood and adolescence) during a particular epoch (say, the Great Depression of the 1930s).

A society reproduces itself continuously, though – babies are born every year, even every day, each with a unique personal length of generation (Ryder 1965:32). The demographic definition of a generation provides no boundaries for saying where one generation stops and the next starts (Kertzer 1983). Ryder preferred the term *cohort* for the alternate idea of people all born together or starting together on some other process such as employment or marriage (a historical generation). Strauss and Howe called such groupings cohort generations: "...cohort generations are to societies what family generations are to families...the earlier generation is always older than the next and normally exercises authority over those that follow – the cohort type in a public setting, the family type in a private setting." (Strauss & Howe 1991:437)

We will refer to a group of people all sharing a common demographic trait (here age or year of birth) as a cohort, as Ryder suggested. However, these cohorts cover short, uniform time periods (single calendar years of birth or five-year ranges) without respect to historical events or conditions.[1] A *historical generation* (the same thing as Strauss and Howe's cohort generation) refers to a group of birth cohorts set off from other groups by strong historical boundaries. What sets apart the people born during a particular span of years (such as the Lucky Few) as a distinct historical generation?

To tell where one historical generation stops and the next begins in calendar time, we must add historical context and events. When biography and history intersect, major historical events and conditions affect people of different ages in different ways. This fact creates historical generations.[2] Ryder's classic study of cohorts and social change (1965) made the important point that the distinctiveness of each historical generation begins with the most elementary fact of size. A large birth cohort faces different options in life from a small one (Easterlin 1966), options that may be affected by historical events but that cannot be ignored or changed once a historical generation has come into existence.

Though we follow the convention of identifying generations in terms of the years when they were born, many of the events that shape the distinctive character of each generation only occur years later. Events taking place as we complete school, find a partner in life, or get a job affect us at young adult ages (Rindfuss, 1991), so Ryder paid attention to unique historical situations as influences on young adults in particular. Dramatic political and economic events such as the stock market crash in 1929, the attack on Pearl Harbor in 1941, the oil shock in the mid 1970s, or the World Trade Center and Pentagon attacks of 2001 changed the ideas and lives of each new generation just coming into adulthood. New safe, inexpensive, reliable contraceptives in the mid 1960s changed the attitudes of people just entering sexual maturity and contemplating whether and when to start families. Sudden changes in immigration laws in the 1920s and again in the 1960s influenced immigrants themselves as well as the communities they left and those where they settled. Traumatic episodes such as war impact young adult ages most, since it is the young who usually fight the wars on the actual battlefields.

Historical epochs and events identify seven generations in the next chapter, quite similar (but not identical) to the generations suggested by Strauss and Howe. We give each generation a name reflecting their most distinctive demographic feature or historical experience, with the generation here called the Lucky Few (the book's namesake generation) just in the middle. Most information in following chapters comes from original calculations using the Integrated Public Use Microdata Samples (IPUMS), publicly-available computerized data files reconstructed from the manuscript decennial Censuses of Population and Housing, and from annual Current Population Surveys available since 1962. This massive effort at data recovery, conducted in recent decades with federal government support, amounts to the demographic equivalent of the Human Genome Project. Taken together, the IPUMS data files map out who we are as a country and how we got that way, allowing us to look at details and patterns that have not been accessible to earlier researchers.

The "stop-motion animation" provided by census data is far from perfect, but it does allow us to see the uniqueness of the Lucky Few in comparison to generations that came before and after them. While census samples let us look at the entire twentieth century, when we to the adult ages of the Lucky Few in the 1970s and later, additional sources of evidence allow us to flesh out the picture more fully. But before taking a closer look at the Lucky Few, the next chapter considers the larger context of successive American generations.

Notes

1. In reserving the term "generation" for individual-level study of kinship Ryder was following the lead of Mannheim (1923, 1927). But philosopher Jose Ortega y Gasset (1923, 1951, 1958) could not have been thinking

of demographic or "family" generations when he suggested that major changes in society occur every fifteen years as one generation replaces another. Other writers also use the term *generation* to describe groups of birth cohorts (Eisenstadt 1956, Carlsson & Karlsson 1970) or people all hired at the same time (Gusfield 1957).

2. Without a doubt, Strauss and Howe remain the reigning champions in drawing boundaries for historical generations, sketching an ambitious panorama of eighteen generations of Americans beginning in the late 1500s. They posit roughly century-long cycles of four repeating generational types, each conditioned by historical experiences during key stages of life. They identify secular crises of social organization and religious awakenings of moral values that alternate every 40–45 years. If we divide life into stages of youth, young adulthood, midlife and elderhood (Strauss & Howe 1991:60), each roughly 20–25 years long, and mark our generations based on such intervals, each religious crisis catches one group in each of the four stages. In the same way, following periods of calm, then secular crisis, then calm, then spiritual crisis again will catch successive other generations at equivalent ages and influence them differently.

"A social moment not only shapes personality according to current phase-of-life roles," suggest Strauss and Howe (1991:444), "but also forges an enduring bond of identity between each cohort-group and its role – an acquired style that redefines both how each group will later regard itself and how it will later be regarded by others." (444)

Strauss & Howe paid most attention to psychological outlooks as expressed in the writings of educated elites in each generation when they decided which historical events to count as "social moments" shaping generations. The present study follows more in the spirit of works like Peter Laslett's Cambridge group, illustrated by his famous *Household and Family in Past Time* (1972), in that we focus on the reconstruction of details of everyday life for the great mass of people in each generation. Since we use different kinds of information for identifying historical periods, the exact dates chosen as generational boundaries in this book differ slightly from those of Strauss and Howe. Still it is interesting to note how similar many of their generational boundaries chosen nearly two decades earlier turn out to be, compared to those derived independently for this analysis.

Chapter 2
American Generations of the Twentieth Century

Contents

Naming the Generations

The Lucky Few form just one of many American generations: some older, some younger. Some historical generations such as the Baby Boomers already have familiar names. We talk about them as recognized groups with special characteristics. Others like the people sometimes called Generation X (or Generation Thirteen by Strauss and Howe) have yet to find a name that really captures their character, even though we recognize them as a historical generation.

The impact of different generations on American life in the twentieth century begins well before the start of the century itself. Generations born before 1900 reached adulthood in the opening years of the century, lived most of their lives during that century, and affected the country in profound ways. The seven generations to be compared throughout this book thus start as far back as the decade following the

E. Carlson, *The Lucky Few*,

© Springer Science+Business Media B.V. 2008

Civil War and cover the entire period from that time to the end of the twentieth century. The seven generations and their birth years are:

1. **New Worlders** (born from 1871 to 1889, median member born in 1880)
2. **Hard Timers** (born from 1890 to 1908, median member born in 1899)
3. **Good Warriors** (born from 1909 to 1928, median member born in 1918)
4. **Lucky Few** (born from 1929 to 1945, median member born in 1937)
5. **Baby Boomers** (born from 1946 to 1964, median member born in 1955)
6. **Generation X** (born from 1965 to 1982, median member born in 1974)
7. **New Boomers** (born from 1983 to 2001, median member born in 1992)

Figure 2.1 shows relative sizes of these generations in U.S. Censuses from 1900 to 2000. The oldest or earliest generation (the New Worlders) appears at the left side of the Figure, and people in each younger generation appear to the right of their elders. Each generation changes in size as successive censuses count its members over the course of their lives. The New Worlders already were present in the 1900 census, but the youngest groups only appear near the end of the century.

Since each generation arrives in society gradually over time, a census only counts a few of its members when they first appear as children. For example, the 1930 Census captured only Lucky Few babies younger than two years old, born in 1929 or early 1930. By 1940 everyone aged eleven or younger belonged to the Lucky Few, but still only about two-thirds of this generation had appeared on the scene. The 1950 Census finally enumerated the whole Lucky Few generation, finding them at ages from 5 to 21.

A generation grows larger with each additional year of births. Counteracting this growth, though, a generation also begins to shrink due to deaths of some of its members even at the very earliest ages. As shown in Fig. 2.2, for example, Good Warriors born between 1909 and 1928 lost about one-fifth of their members (nearly ten million children) between birth and age fifteen due to the high risk of infant and

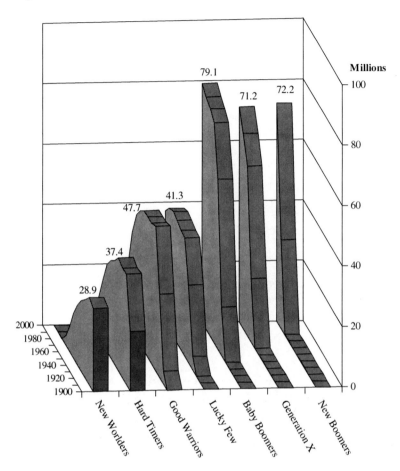

Fig. 2.1 U.S. generations by size (with maximums) from decennial census counts
Source: Original tabulations from Census Public Use Microdata Samples.

child deaths early in the century. That generation then hardly changed in size from age fifteen to age thirty or from age thirty to age forty-five, as net immigration made up for further mortality.

On the other hand, Baby Boomers born from 1946 to 1964 came into the world later in the century when risk of infant and child deaths had fallen dramatically. Figure 2.2 shows that from birth to age fifteen the Baby Boomer generation lost hardly any members. Then from age fifteen to age thirty they gained an additional five million members, because new immigrants outnumbered the few deaths of young adults.

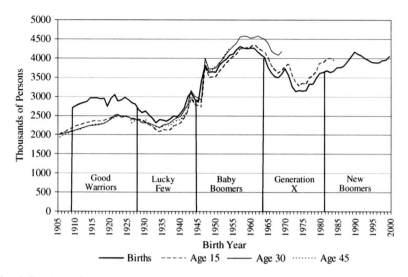

Fig. 2.2 Size of generations over the early life course
Source: U.S. Bureau of the Census (selected years). Estimates of the Population of the United States. Series P-25, selected numbers.

The Baby Boomers show us how a generation can grow by immigration even after the years of its births have passed.

As a generation reaches midlife (after four or five census counts–see Fig. 2.1 above) advancing age begins to magnify the effect of mortality. Death whittles away the members of the group faster and faster. Eventually the generation passes through the oldest ages and disappears. This extinction already has happened to the oldest generation we consider, the New Worlders born between 1871 and 1889. Even the youngest member of this generation would have been one hundred and eleven years old in the 2000 census. The Hard Timers born between 1890 and 1908 are rapidly reaching the same point. The youngest of them passed age ninety-two in the 2000 Census, and the oldest would have been one hundred and ten years old. Eventually every generation disappears.

To take a closer look at the historical generations who have shaped and have been shaped by the twentieth century in the United States, we consider each of them in turn. We begin with people reaching adulthood as the century began.

New Worlders (Born from 1871 to 1889)

The earliest generation considered here includes children born between 1871 and 1889, that is, from Reconstruction until the closing of the western frontier. We look no further back in history than this generation, and call them New Worlders because so many of them immigrated to the New World from other continents. Strauss and Howe (1991:233) chose wider and slightly different boundaries (1860–1882) for their roughly-equivalent Missionary generation. As with any attempt at grouping people in society, different studies with different perspectives and aims may choose varying generational boundaries – Chapter 1 above provided the framework that led to choices made in defining these seven generations.

While the New Worlders completed their appearance as a generation, 40 million Americans grew to 63 million by 1890, increasing by more than half in just twenty years. Fifteen of the 23 million new Americans represented natural increase, the difference between nearly 30 million New Worlder births and about 15 million people who died during the 1870s and 1880s. The other one-third (eight million people) arrived as immigrants from other lands, part of the last great wave of unrestricted immigration into the United States. By 1890, New York City held twice as many Irish people as Dublin and as many Germans as Hamburg.

The New Worlders lived in dynamic, exciting times–years that brought the world's first National Park (Yellowstone Park established in 1872), the first Kentucky Derby (run in 1875), professional baseball's National League (formed in 1876), Alexander Graham Bell's telephone (1876), Thomas Edison's phonograph (1877) and light bulb (1878), and George Eastman's Kodak camera using rolls of film (1888). In 1889, as the final birth cohort of the New Worlder generation arrived on the scene, newspaper reporter Nellie Bly (one of the earliest examples of a "media personality") made a real trip *Around the World in 72 Days* (Bly 1890) besting the fictional eighty-day adventure penned by Jules Verne.

Construction began in 1874 on a gift from France, the Statue of Liberty in New York harbor. An inscription at its base reads, "Give me your tired, your poor, your huddled masses, yearning to breathe free. I lift my torch beside the golden door." These huddled masses, the millions of immigrants coming to America, provide the key to understanding the special character of New Worlders as a generation. Many landed by ship in east coast seaports such as New York, where they could glimpse the Statue of Liberty and her motto. During the first two decades of the twentieth century more than fifteen million immigrants arrived in the United States. Such a flood of arrivals meant that the censuses of 1910 and 1920 counted more than one of every seven persons in the United States as born in some other country—the highest share recorded for any of our 20th century censuses.

Young adults made up an overwhelming share of these immigrants, as is usual for international migration, and New Worlders found themselves squarely in the heart of the immigrating ages just in time to absorb the wave of foreign-born arrivals. By the time their generation reached its maximum size (by about the time of the 1920 Census) nearly *one of every four* New Worlders was foreign-born (see Fig. 2.3), giving them something that disappeared from later American generations for most of the twentieth century—a very large proportion of people who knew first-hand what it meant *not* to be an American (at least not by birth), who in many cases had struggled very hard to become one, and who had succeeded.

We draw the upper bound for births of New Worlders at 1889 because the 1890 Census reported the closing of the western frontier. Settlement had become so general across the whole continent that any frontier had ceased to exist. Frederick Jackson Turner, in his famous 1893 essay on the closing of the frontier, suggested that this change marked a turning point in the whole spirit and attitude of the country. We will accept this notion, and start a new historical generation with the date of the census announcement.

New Worlders as a group lived differently in many ways from generations that followed. For example, as they were reaching adulthood in 1900, about one-third of all New Worlders lived on farms. Even forty years later, as they approached the end of their working lives, between one-fourth and one-fifth of this generation still remained on farms. When younger generations moved off the farms and into cities, they left many of the New Worlders behind in rural areas.

Later in their lives, New Worlders became the first American generation to benefit from the introduction of a national system of social insurance. Ida May Fuller, a legal secretary born in Vermont in

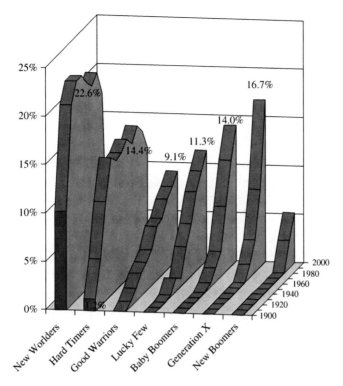

Fig. 2.3 Percent foreign-born (with maximums) by generation and census year
Source: Original calculations from Census Public Use Microdata Samples.

1875, started paying Social Security withholding taxes in 1937. In 1939 she retired and collected the very first regular Social Security check (for $22.54, which roughly paid back the entire $24.75 she paid into the system during her last two years of employment). Since she lived to be 100 years old, by 1975 Ida May Fuller eventually collected $22,888.92 in benefits – a thousand dollars for every dollar she had paid into the system.

New Worlders continued retiring through the years of the Great Depression and the Second World War, years when the Lucky Few were just being born. By 2000, New Worlders had passed completely out of the upper ages of the population. Today that generation is all but extinct. Throughout their lives, this generation managed to remain unique as the most foreign-born generation of the 20th century.

Hard Timers (Born from 1890 to 1908)

Our second generation includes people born between 1890 and 1908, that is, from the closing of the frontier to the end of Theodore Roosevelt's second term as President. This generation stands with one foot in the 19th century and the other in the 20th century. We call them the Hard Timers. The hard times that give them their name included a world war, a disastrous economic depression, and then another world war, a string of calamities that all but smothered the adult lives of this entire generation. For different reasons Strauss and Howe (1991:247) called the people born between 1883 and 1900 the Lost generation, but a sense of powerlessness and missing out on things in life appears in their description, as well.

The population of the United States swelled from 63 million people in 1890 to 92 million by 1910. More than forty percent of that increase came from immigrants, often arriving to join the New Worlder generation as described above. The other sixty percent represented natural increase (the difference between Hard Timer births and the deaths in the United States during the same years) and also the inclusion of people already living in territories that became new states. Between 1890 and 1908 Idaho, Oklahoma, Utah and Wyoming joined the Union as the westward movement of the population continued.

Americans like writer Ernest Hemmingway, jazz legend Duke Ellington or mobster Al Capone, all born in 1899 at the heart of the Hard Timer generation, reached age eighteen in 1917 as the United States finally entered the First World War. In that last fierce year from 1917 to the Armistice in 1918, the United States drafted three million Americans under the Selective Service Act passed by Congress. Nearly five million Americans in all served during the war, and since Hard Timers occupied all ages between 10 and 28 in 1918, most of the combat troops were young Hard Timer men.

In the trench warfare on Europe's Western Front, Hard Timer soldiers encountered first-hand the industrial-scale slaughter that new weapons caused among troops in old-fashioned, close-packed formations. More than 116,000 American soldiers died as a result of the First World War, but over half of these deaths resulted from disease and infection rather than battle.

The Great War gave the first hint of the adult lives in store for Hard Timers. At war's end soldiers came back to civilian lives and to the economic frenzy that today we call the Roaring Twenties. For a few years after the armistice was signed, Hard Timers had a chance to find civilian jobs, to marry and start families, and to catch up on normal lives. The opportunity, however, proved to be short-lived. Hard Timers had the bad luck to occupy all ages from 21 to 39 when the stock market crashed in 1929, so the impact of the Great Depression fell hardest on them. Not everyone in this generation lost a job or failed to find one, but the economic impact devastated the lives of a whole generation. In 1926 only 801,000 persons were unemployed and looking for work, less than two percent of a civilian labor force of almost 46 million workers. By 1930 this total swelled to 4,300,000 unemployed, and in 1933 at the depths of the Depression the total reached nearly 13 million people, one-fourth of the entire civilian labor force. Since young Hard Timers had the least experience and job security, their unemployment rates rose even higher.

Unemployment rates never dropped below ten percent of the labor force until 1941, the year that the Japanese bombed Pearl Harbor. Thus when mass unemployment eventually loosened its grip on the throats of many Hard Timers and their families, they immediately found themselves caught up in the global conflagration of the Second World War. That war was fought predominantly by the next generation described below, but the Hard Timers at home felt the impact of wartime through government freezes on wages, salaries and prices. In 1943 a government edict even froze 27 million workers in their jobs for the duration of the war—a simple statement, but staggering to think about for generations who never experienced such regimentation.

All these hardships meant that Hard Timers had dramatically fewer children than previous generations of Americans. Jeanne Clare Ridley and her colleagues (Dawson et al. 1980) studied a national sample of Hard Timer women (see International Consortium for Political and Social Research Study #4698) to explore how they managed to have so few children, long before the contraceptive revolution that came decades later. Ironically, these low birth rates of the Hard Timers during the Great Depression give us our first glimpse of the book's namesake generation, the Lucky Few – they are these few children beginning to appear during the Depression.

Apart from a few years in the 1920s, the Hard Timer generation spent almost their entire working lives first fighting a World War, then coping with the dislocations of the Great Depression, and finally fitting themselves into the highly-regulated hothouse environment of another wartime economy. By the time the postwar economic boom got underway, the oldest Hard Timers already had begun to retire. They may have enjoyed the fewest opportunities and the smallest range of choices about the direction of their lives of any American generation in the twentieth century.

Good Warriors (Born from 1909 to 1928)

Our third generation began to appear in 1909 (the year after Teddy Roosevelt left office) and continued to arrive through 1928 (the year before the 1929 stock market crash began the Great Depression). They star in Tom Brokaw's popular account (1998) of *The Greatest Generation*. We call this generation born between 1909 and 1928 the Good Warriors, because this one generation essentially did the fighting for the United States in the Second World War. More than for any other war in U.S. history, Americans agree that in the Second World War they fought on the right side in a battle of good against evil, a Just War fought for good purposes and ending in clear victory. This definition persists, defining not only the war itself but the soldiers who fought it. By fighting in the Good War they became the Good Warriors, in their own eyes and in the eyes of the rest of the country. The image remains strong to this day. It defined an entire generation for the rest of their lives. Strauss and Howe (1991:261) simply refer to them as the G.I. generation, marking their boundaries at 1901 and 1924.

However, the experiences that bound the Good Warriors together and marked them for life did not begin with war. The oldest of them reached age 19 and the youngest had just been born at the time of the 1929 stock market crash. Good Warrior children watched their parents losing jobs rather than losing jobs of their own, but they certainly witnessed the Great Depression first-hand.

By 1942 the Good Warriors occupied ages 14–33, monopolizing the main ages of military service. They served on the front lines in the deserts of Africa, the hedgerows of Europe, and the jungles of Asia and the Pacific. When it was all over, 16 million men had seen active duty during wartime—almost four times the number of Americans who had fought in the First World War. The Good Warrior generation totaled only about 22 million men altogether during the war years, so even allowing for officers and other older soldiers who might have included a few Hard Timers, over two-thirds of the entire Good Warrior male population spent at least part of the war in military uniforms. These estimates tally very closely with the percent of Good Warrior men who reported themselves as veterans in post-war census counts, as discussed in detail in Chapter 5.

The almost 58 million Good Warrior children born between 1909 and 1928 also grew up to be the most native-born generation in American history. The millions of immigrants who joined earlier generations in young adulthood simply failed to materialize in this generation. Restrictive immigration laws shut down the flow of immigrants in the 1920s. The Great Depression kept them out during the 1930s. When the Good Warriors marched off to fight the Second World War, less than one in twenty of their generation had been born outside the country (compared to almost one of every four New Worlders or one of every eight Hard Timers). Restrictive immigration laws remained in place for nearly half a century, so even when the youngest Good Warrior was 72 years old in 2000 (see Fig. 2.3), less than ten percent of people in this generation were foreign-born. Having everyone born in the same country, growing up with the same schoolbooks and sports and newspaper headlines, must always be remembered when trying to understand the distinctiveness of this generation. Native-born homogeneity rivals their role as the winners of the Good War in defining the Good Warriors.

After the war a peacetime economic boom transformed the lives of the Good Warrior generation. Still at ages 17–36 at war's end, many remained young enough to begin families. They helped to invent the new automobile suburbs that came to symbolize postwar America. They became parents of some of the Baby Boomers. Unlike the Hard Timers, Good Warriors had enough time left after their war to switch gears, to go from hardship and lack of choices to unexpected opportunities in their careers and family lives. If any twentieth-century generation of Americans could adopt the motto "better late than never" as their own, it would be the Good Warriors. This generation, with its native-born homogeneity, its early taste of harsh economic facts of life, and the patriotic spirit springing from wartime military service, has taken a unique place in American history. For example, every President of the United States starting from the election of John Kennedy in 1962 (except Lyndon Johnson, born in 1908 and so one year too old) belonged to the Good Warrior generation, until Baby Boomers Bill Clinton and George W. Bush were elected near the end of the century.

Lucky Few (Born from 1929 to 1945)

After the disrupted lives of the Hard Timer generation and the patriotic lives of the Good Warriors, we come to the Lucky Few themselves. They have been the least-noticed generation of the century, though mentioned by a few writers such as Strauss and Howe (1991:279), who chose birth year boundaries 1925–1942 rather than 1929–1945 for the group they called the Silent generation. Lancaster and Stillman's (2002) book, *When Generations Collide*, lumps together both Good Warriors and the Lucky Few as "traditionalists," which is an accurate description, but chapters below show clearly that the Lucky Few form a very special generation, not to be confused with either the Good Warriors before them or the Baby Boomers after them.

For the earliest of the Lucky Few, life did not look so lucky at first. These first babies were born in 1929, the year of the Wall Street crash and the beginning of the slide into the Great Depression. In the depths of the Depression unemployment swept like a wildfire through the homes of their Hard Timer parents. Then as the clouds of war gathered yet again beyond the Atlantic and Pacific oceans, Franklin Roosevelt and the Congress began to build up American military forces. By 1939 war broke out in Europe. For two years the United States balanced awkwardly on its neutrality but in 1941 the massive Japanese naval air raid on Pearl Harbor finally tipped the scales. Millions of Lucky Few children saw their Good Warrior parents ship out to fight in distant lands. For the first half of the 1940s the Second World War overshadowed all other facts of life in America. Many Lucky Few children born to Americans of Japanese ancestry (such as *Star Trek's* George Takei or Pat Morita of *The Karate Kid* movie fame) found themselves interned along with their parents in isolated camps.

Whether influenced by depression or war, Lucky Few children all have childhood memories formed during unusual and difficult historical times. But in 1945 these early clouds cleared away. The Lucky Few generation ended with the last year of wartime births in 1945, before the explosion of the Baby Boom. Figure 2.2 above shows the remarkably low number of births counted during this period, totaling only about 44 million in all the years from 1929 to 1945 – almost one-third fewer than births of the Good Warrior generation before them. Though infant and child death rates were falling at mid-century, early losses among the Lucky Few meant that in adulthood, this generation barely exceeded 40 million members (see Fig. 2.1).

Immigrant origins marked the New Worlders as unique. Economic limitations shaped the Hard Timers, and military service dominated the formative years of the Good Warriors. The simple demographic fact of generation size, however, has dominated the lives of the Lucky Few. Reinforcing their small generation size, immigration did little more to expand the Lucky Few generation in adulthood (see Fig. 2.3) than had been true for the Good Warriors. Legal barriers, economic depression and war restricted immigration to a bare trickle through the 1930s, 1940s and 1950s. Similarly to the Good Warriors, the Lucky Few counted only a little over ten percent of their number as foreign-born even late in life, and the share had been much smaller for most of their lives.

The oldest members of the Lucky Few reached age sixteen as Germany and Japan surrendered, and Lucky Few children suddenly saw life change drastically. Their median members born in 1937 could look forward to a decade of peace and plenty before becoming the high school graduating class of 1955 – a group including future movie star Jane Fonda (attending the exclusive Emma Willard School in Troy, New York), future discount broker Charles Schwab (growing up as the son of a lawyer in California), future actor Warren Beatty (a football star at Washington-Lee High School in Arlington, Virginia), or future General Colin Powell (living with his Jamaican immigrant parents in the South Bronx).

Most of the Lucky Few were too young to serve in the Korean War in the early 1950s (but see Chapter 5 for the oldest of them, who did fight in that conflict). They were not too young, however, to take advantage of the longest economic boom in the nation's history. In fact, they were positioned perfectly for it. Unemployment rates for young workers reached historic low levels during the 1950s and 1960s. Employers competed fiercely for the few available young employees, driving up wages and accelerating promotions up the career ladder. While nearly universal wartime military service unified young men in the Good Warrior generation, young men in the Lucky Few generation experienced nearly universal peacetime employment.

The Lucky Few began to realize just how lucky they were. Despite more schooling than had been achieved by the Good Warriors, the Lucky Few also married far earlier than any other generation in the twentieth century. They began having babies at such a pace that these years became known as the era of "motherhood mania." At the peak of the early marriage trend in 1958 (when the Lucky Few occupied ages 12–29) the average age of brides marrying for the first time dropped below age twenty.

Since they found themselves bringing up the Baby Boom, since their husbands were doing so amazingly well in their jobs, and since economic roles for women were just beginning to change, most women in the Lucky Few generation kept a lower profile in the labor force during their early lives than did the men. Once their children began to grow up, however, Lucky Few women also began working for pay (further boosting family incomes). While no more than half of the women in the Good Warrior generation ever held paying jobs at any one time, nearly two-thirds of all women in the Lucky Few generation were employed by the time they reached their forties and fifties.

The other side of this coin of economic prosperity meant that Lucky Few men could retire earlier than previous generations. In retirement, the Lucky Few found themselves drawing unprecedented levels of pensions and other support from the massive Baby Boom generation behind them, and living longer and in better health than any previous generation in history.

Baby Boomers (Born from 1946 to 1964)

By virtue of its massive size, the familiar Baby Boom generation long ago shouldered its way past academics, government bureaucrats and eager marketing executives to capture the attention of the mass media and the imagination of the American public. Strauss and Howe join virtually every other writer on generations in recent decades in calling them "Boomers."

With the end of the Second World War, millions of American soldiers returned home and the birth rate suddenly leaped upward. In 1946 the Total Fertility Rate or TFR (a standard measure of childbearing) jumped by more than ten percent, surpassing three births per woman over a reproductive lifetime. The TFR remained above 3.0 for the next 18 years, defining the conventional boundaries of the Baby Boom. In 1964 the TFR dropped by more than ten percent, to a level below 3.0 for the first time in the postwar era. Almost 76 million babies were born in the United States during the eighteen years from 1946 to 1964 nearly double the 44 million Lucky Few births.

Unique events and conditions reinforced the demographic distinctiveness of the American Baby Boom, defining it as a historical generation. Baby Boomers grew up in an era of unprecedented prosperity— the period in which their Lucky Few parents (and some of the youngest Good Warriors, getting a late start on family life) attained the good life and shared it with their children. Not all Americans shared equally in the postwar prosperity, however. Even though the Supreme Court ruled in 1954 in *Brown v. Board of Education of Topeka* that segregated schools were inherently unequal, cities and states resisted school integration fiercely. Lucky Few member Martin Luther King and the NAACP led a 1955 boycott of city buses in Montgomery, Alabama. Baby Boomer children attending schools in Little Rock, Arkansas watched National Guard troops called out by President Eisenhower protecting the first black students to enroll in Central High in 1957.

When the first Baby Boomers graduated in the high school class of 1962, they faced another historical event that marked them as a generation. Escalation of the Vietnam conflict came just in time to transport them (along with a few of the youngest of the Lucky Few) into combat in the jungles of that southeast-Asian nation. The Vietnam conflict affected American society very differently from the Second World War. Americans fought in a vicious guerrilla conflict alongside half-hearted and often corrupt local allies. The first television war in American history intruded on families at dinner every evening with continual scenes of bloodied men lifted urgently into waiting helicopters. Vietnam did not begin well, and it did not end well.

Baby Boomers who fought in Vietnam came home to an alienating environment devoid of victory parades and hero-worship. Those who resisted and protested the war became even more alienated from older generations by the very fact of that resistance. Both of the

Baby Boomer Presidents elected at the end of the twentieth century (William Jefferson Clinton and George W. Bush) had to come to terms with the ambivalent character of Vietnam, and the resulting ambivalence that each man's personal relationship to that war generated in the American public. The Second World War may have been the Good War, but Vietnam in some respects became its opposite— a source of division rather than unity, a conflict the United States clearly did *not* win, an ongoing memory tinged with confusion more than pride. Whether they fought in the war or against the war, then, Baby Boomers came out of the Vietnam experience in the early 1970s facing a generation gap at least as large as any seen in recent history.

Their teeming numbers (coupled with the sudden economic slump triggered by oil price shocks in the mid-1970s) destined Baby Boom men to experience the most dismal career progress since the Hard Timers encountered the Great Depression in the 1930s. As Valerie K. Oppenheimer (1982) has illustrated, this meant more unemployment and lower wage gains for Boomer men. At the same time, Baby Boom women achieved advances in education beyond the dreams of earlier generations, and then poured into the work force in unprecedented numbers – partly offsetting the unusually slow progress of men in their generation.

Economic troubles of Baby Boom men combined with the economic progress won by Baby Boom women dramatically slowed family formation, shifting both marriages and childbearing to later ages. These dynamic trends are aptly drawn in Richard Easterlin's *Birth and Fortune*, the most popular demographic description of the Baby Boomers and their tribulations. Taken all together, the historical and demographic influences enumerated above certainly have molded the Baby Boomers into another distinctive generation of the twentieth century.

Generation X (Born from 1965 to 1982)

If the Baby Boom ended with 1964, the last year with more than four million U.S. births, what came after it? This newer question has received less attention, perhaps in part because the new generation born

in 1965 and after was smaller than the Baby Boom. The second down-
turn in births shown in Fig. 2.2 reached a low point in 1975, when
only a little over three million births were recorded. After that year
birth totals gradually recovered and by the early 1980s again began to
rival the numbers observed during the Baby Boom. For this reason,
we set the upper bound on the post-Baby Boom generation at the end
of 1982. The years from 1965 to 1982 yielded only 62 million births
in the United States. Just as the Lucky Few fell short of the birth totals
for the Good Warriors, this new generation fell short of the birth totals
from the Baby Boom years.

Demographers called these years the Baby Bust (Dunn 1993). Per-
plexed marketing specialists who couldn't think of any other name
simply took to calling these people Generation X, and that label with
all its implications of confusion and alienation has persisted. Strauss
and Howe (1991:317) apparently could not think of a good name, either, since they simply referred to people born between 1961 and 1981
as "Generation Thirteen" – the least descriptive of any of the eighteen
generational names they selected. Based on the demographic common
ground of fewer births, we apply the market researchers' Generation
X label to people born between 1965 and 1982, but following chapters
dispel a lot of the mystery about this generation.

One feature of Generation X actually links them back to earlier
generations like the New Worlders or the Hard Timers. Even more
importantly, this aspect of Generation X also increased its size even
after all the members had been born. After half a century of severe restrictions on entry into the country, U.S. immigration laws
changed again dramatically in the mid-1960s. Another wave of immigration began to build up in the country at the end of the twentieth century, even larger than the wave a hundred years earlier. From
slightly over three million legal immigrants during the 1960s, the
totals climbed to more than four million arrivals during the 1970s,
then to nearly six and a half million during the 1980s and almost ten
million during the 1990s (and these totals do not even include illegal
immigrants).

The earliest immigrants in this new wave actually joined the Baby
Boomers, but Generation X felt the impact more strongly. Censuses
probably under-count illegal aliens present in the country, so census figures provide a conservative estimate of immigrant impact.
Still, when the 2000 Census counted Generation X between ages

seventeen and thirty-five (see Fig. 2.3) one in every six of them had been born outside the United States. No one can understand Generation X without pondering the implications of this return to a pattern not seen since the lives of the New Worlders and Hard Timers at the beginning of the twentieth century. This time, though, it is diversity with a difference.

In the early 1900s most foreign-born New Worlders and Hard Timers came from Italy, Poland, Greece, Ireland, Germany, Scandinavia, the British Isles, and other countries in Europe. By contrast, the 2000 Census traced most foreign-born Generation Xers (59 percent) to origins in Latin America. Two-thirds of these Latino immigrants in Generation X (nearly half a million persons) came from Mexico alone. The second-largest group of Generation X immigrants, amounting to 22 percent, arrived from Asia – especially India, China, the Philippines, Vietnam and Korea in that order. Only about one in ten immigrants came from anywhere in Europe, and these usually came from Germany, Russia, or the former communist countries in eastern Europe. The rest of the world contributed the remaining eight percent of Generation X immigrants.

After the first Generation Xers started high school in 1979, American hostages in Iran filled the news and the nation elected Ronald Reagan to the presidency. No sudden economic swings or major wars with massive casualties turned society on its head in the following years. A new conservative trend dominated American politics and, as shown in Chapter 7, affected Generation Xers during their formative ages. Tax cuts produced windfall gains in income for the wealthiest Americans during the 1980s, but the economy failed to follow the publicized predictions of the supply-side economists who designed the scenario. Instead, massive federal deficits ballooned upward, paralyzing government initiatives and creating a drag on the economy. Wages for people at the lower end of the scale stagnated. The gap between the "haves" and the "have-nots" grew visibly wider before the eyes of the young members of Generation X as they progressed through high school and university ages.

Marriages, already delayed and avoided by the Baby Boomers, continued to be delayed and avoided by Generation X. Birth rates also remained low. If being in a small generation brings inherent advantages, as we will suggest for the Lucky Few in the following chapters, will this also turn out to be true in the long run for Generation X?

Will they eventually turn out to be *another* Lucky Few, when we are able to look back with the clearer hindsight of history? Or does it take a combination of both small generation size and favorable historical, economic and political events to give rise to a truly lucky generation? The final chapter of the book explores this question.

New Boomers (Born from 1983 to 2001)

Even before advertising executives and marketing experts began to get a grip on Generation X, another generation already had materialized in our kindergartens and day care centers. Between 1983 and 2001 the number of births in the United States rebounded once again. This time, however, the resurgence of births did not stem from anything like an era of "motherhood mania" characterized by younger ages of marriage or increased childbearing at young ages. The resurgence of births simply reflected the fact that the huge Baby Boom generation began having their own children at last. Although it took them longer than the Lucky Few to get started, the Boomers produced an "echo" of births that nearly matched their own numbers. A continuing tide of immigration in the early 21st century means that this newest generation eventually may even outnumber the original Baby Boom by a solid margin – for this reason, and because they are still so young, no maximum percent foreign-born for them appears in Fig. 2.3.

We call people born between 1983 and 2001 the New Boomer generation for this reason. Strauss and Howe begin their almost-equivalent generation, which they called simply the Millennials (Howe & Strauss 2000), in 1982. Our upper bound in 2001 reflects several simultaneous boundary events. Political and social changes altered the social fabric of American society after the tragedy of the September 11th terrorist attacks, and persistent economic difficulties rooted in issues of energy and the environment also began to manifest themselves in the early years of the new century. The resulting slowdown in birth rates and generation size marks the end of the New Boomer generation.

For New Boomers, Vietnam appeared alongside the Second World War as a lesson in school books, not a personal memory. They grew up witnessing military operations resembling Teddy Roosevelt's imperialistic adventures a century earlier, rather than the titanic struggles that engulfed the entire nation in mid-century—episodes such as the invasion of Grenada to oust pro-Cuban Marxist rebels in 1983, or intrigues such as the shady Iran/Contra dealings of Colonel Oliver North providing secret support to anti-Marxist rebels in Nicaragua.

Terrorists occupied public attention almost continuously throughout the childhoods of the New Boomers, who witnessed the bombing of the U.S. Embassy and the Marine headquarters in Lebanon in 1983. Hijackings of a TWA flight in Athens and the cruise ship Achille Lauro followed, along with bomb attacks in the Rome and Vienna airports, all in 1985. A string of other bombings later in the decade culminated in the crash of a Pan American flight from London to New York in Lockerbie, Scotland in 1988, the year that President Reagan's vice president George H. W. Bush was elected to the White House.

Then in 1990 Saddam Hussein invaded Kuwait and threatened to take control of even more of the oil in the Middle East than he already controlled in Iraq. By the end of the year, 485,000 troops from 17 countries had massed in Saudi Arabia and neighboring countries. Twelve of the 21 member countries of the Arab League had condemned the takeover of Kuwait. The Persian Gulf conflict in 1991 lasted about as long as the Spanish-American War in 1898, and only hundreds rather than thousands or tens of thousands of U.S. soldiers died.

At home, a resurgent U.S. economy generated tens of millions of new jobs. Federal budget deficits shrank rapidly and then actually reversed to budget surpluses at the end of the 1990s. Scientists announced that they had completed mapping the human genome that year, and the Euro went into circulation as the new currency of a unifying European economy.

On September 11th, 2001, terrorists from Saudi Arabia and other countries hijacked several airliners simultaneously inside the United States, and rather than simply bombing the planes or making demands, crashed the planes into the World Trade Center in New York City and the Pentagon in Washington DC. After that date, the United States changed fundamentally as a society, making it the logical point for drawing the upper limit of the last American generation born in the twentieth century.

Comparing Generations

With seven generations sketched against the historical context that shaped and defined each of them, the stage is set for a more detailed look at the Lucky Few. On some issues in the remaining chapters, we only will be able to compare them to earlier generations because the younger generations have not reached those points in life yet. On other issues we only will be able to compare them to the latest generations, because relevant measures of some aspects of life simply are not available for the oldest generations. Set in the midst of these other generations, however, we will be able to see the Lucky Few in systematic perspective, and thus gain a better appreciation for their uniqueness.

In Chapter 3 on childhood and schooling of each generation, Good Warrior and Lucky Few children enjoy the highest share of stable parental families in U.S. history and young Lucky Few men make the single largest leap forward in educational attainment of any considered group. Chapter 4 shows young Lucky Few men reaching the highest level of early career employment ever recorded, and together with their wives, marrying earlier and having more children than either the Good Warriors before them or the Baby Boomers after them. Chapter 5 continues the story of good fortune as Lucky Few men serve nearly as often in the military as the Good Warriors, but with the important difference that most such service came in peacetime. Twice as many of the Lucky Few compared to younger Baby Boomers qualify for veterans' benefits, but wartime casualties of the Lucky Few reached less than a tenth of the losses experienced by the Good Warriors. In Chapter 6, Lucky Few men make the biggest jump of the century into professional, managerial and other white-collar occupations, even as Lucky Few women become more concentrated in the "pink-collar ghetto" of clerical work than any other generation in history. The Lucky Few also scored big advances as a generation investing in corporate stocks, and may be the last generation with widespread access to defined-benefit pension plans. Unlike earlier generations, they gradually moved away from labor unions as they left blue-collar jobs behind. A range of public opinion issues explored in Chapter 7 reveals the Lucky Few as the most politically polarized generation of the century. Chapter 8 looks within this unique generation to uncover important differences in education, lifetime migration, family formation and other key life events between black and white members of the Lucky Few. Chapter 9 shows remarkable advances among the Lucky Few in chances of survival, along with strong gains in avoiding disability in old age – both part of a larger century-long pattern. An important part of these gains can be traced to steady improvement in the ratio of employed workers to dependents in the U.S. population over the century, enabling both men and women in the Lucky Few to enjoy historic high levels of independence and good health in later life. Finally, Chapter 10 compares this small and fortunate generation to the other small generation of the century (Generation X) and shows that generation size by itself is not enough to guarantee prosperity for any group of Americans. The good fortune enjoyed by the Lucky Few throughout their lives stands revealed, in the final analysis, as a synergy combining their sparse numbers with a whole series of favorable historical circumstances.

Chapter 3
Unlikely Origins

Contents

The last place anyone would begin looking for the luckiest generation in U.S. history probably would be the depths of the Great Depression in the 1930s, but that is precisely where the Lucky Few first turn up. Low birth rates caused by hard times produced the first generation in the nation's history with fewer people than the generation before them. In this chapter we concentrate on the Lucky Few when they were children, when home and family dominated their lives. We consider in particular the impact of economic depression and wartime on these childhoods, and then compare schooling for different generations.

From Farms to Cities

Our starting point concerns an important change in the surroundings where these childhoods unfolded. As Fig. 3.1 illustrates, at the dawn of the 20th century over 40 percent of Hard Timer children under age ten lived on farms. (The share was even higher, over 50 percent, for New Worlder children in the late 19th century – not shown.)

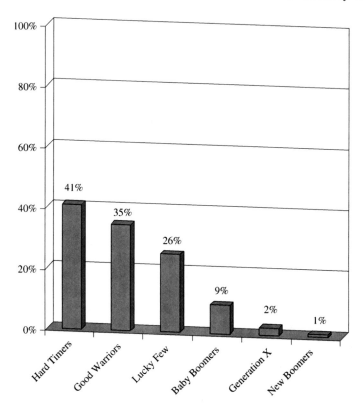

Fig. 3.1 Children living on farms by generation
Source: Original calculations from Census Public Use Microdata Samples.

We focus on children's lives before their tenth birthdays because
this gives us a snapshot of childhood ages when home and family
shape our lives, and also because censuses come every ten years. Since
each of our generations spans more than ten years of birth cohorts, we
can never see a whole generation of children at ages under ten in a
single census. We count children in one census or another at ages less
than ten years old, but we must stitch together data from more than
one census to capture all the members of any generation. For example,
Lucky Few births from 1929 and 1930 appear in the 1930 Census at
ages zero and one, but are older than ten in all later censuses. Births
from 1931 to 1940 appear at ages 0–9 in the 1940 Census. Then we
observe the last Lucky Few children born from 1941 to 1945 at ages
5–9 in the 1950 Census. All three of these groups combine to produce
the 26 percent of all Lucky Few children living on farms shown in
Fig. 3.1.

Over the course of the 20th century, the U.S. farm population virtually disappeared. Migration to cities encompassed all ages, leaving fewer families on farms. Compared to 40 percent of all Hard Timer children counted on farms, only a little over one-third of Good Warriors had similar childhoods. Even the one-fourth of Lucky Few children who started life on farms dwindled away to nearly nothing by the time their generation reached retirement ages at the end of the century. Only one in ten Baby Boomers were counted on farms in childhood. Generation X and the New Boomers missed virtually all of the urban transformation of the twentieth century, and had little chance to experience farm living as anything to do with everyday life. For most of them farms represented only exotic, hypothetical places on a par with South Sea islands or Egyptian pyramids, or perhaps a place where they might visit an elderly relative on rare occasions. Only one or two percent of them were ever counted by a census as children living on farms.

Rise and Fall of "Normal" Households

Peter Uhlenberg (1974) noted great historical variation in the ability of Americans to live up to the ideal of a married mother and father in an independent household with their children. He pointed to the mid-twentieth century as the time when American society was most successful at achieving this ideal. People married earlier than ever before. Divorces happened more rarely than today. Few spouses died young, leaving widows or widowers behind. Most couples had children. In short, families all across the United States looked more alike and matched people's idealized images of family life more than ever before or since.

While Uhlenberg considered this high-tide of family life from the perspective of adults, Hernandez (1993) came to much the same conclusion from the perspective of American children. Childhoods around mid-century coincided more than ever with intact nuclear family life. In this chapter, we re-visit both perspectives of adults and of children under the age of ten, considering them in terms of the seven generations that form the subject of this book. We start by looking at things through the eyes of the children themselves.

The vertical bars in Fig. 3.2 confirm that the great majority of children in every generation lived with both parents before their tenth birthdays. However, important fractions of children also found themselves living with only their mothers, or with only their fathers, or even with neither parent present in the home. Most of the children in earlier generations shown living with neither parent in Fig. 3.2 lived with grandparents. For example, Lucky Few comedienne Carol Burnett moved with her grandmother from San Antonio, Texas to California while still a young child. She grew up in her grandmother's home, which positioned her to attend Hollywood High School and UCLA, helping to explain how she found a career in theatre and television.

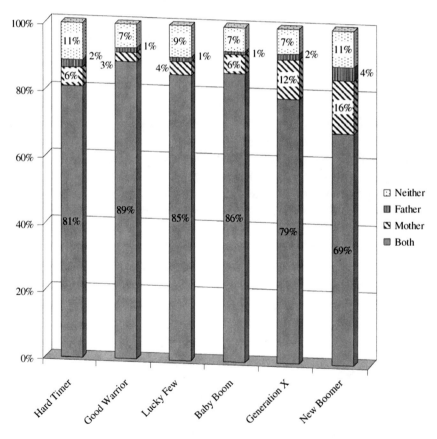

Fig. 3.2 Parents in children's households
Source: Original calculations from IPUMS Census samples.

Death rates were higher at the beginning of the 20th century. As Uhlenberg (1974) notes, higher death rates meant more widowed parents and even orphans for our first two generations. Eleven percent of Hard Timer children under ten lived in a home missing both parents (living instead with a grandparent or other relative) and another eight percent lived with only one parent. Only 81 percent of Hard Timer children lived with both parents.

Later generations of children, however, show us exactly what Uhlenberg and Hernandez both described. Almost 90 percent children under ten in the Good Warrior generation lived with both their parents when captured by census counts around mid-century. Together with the Lucky Few and the Baby Boomers, Good Warriors lived their childhoods during the high tide of idealized family structure in American history.

Since that time, despite continued improvements in survival, the high tide of two-parent homes has ebbed. Rising rates of single parenthood and divorce outweigh survival gains made by parents, increasing the exposure of younger generations of children to alternative family contexts. While the most common alternative to both parents at the start of the 20th century involved living with grandparents, by the end of the century living with an unmarried mother had become the most common alternative instead. Each new generation of children since the Baby Boom has lost ground in terms of the two-parent ideal. Generation X children were less likely to live with both parents than any of the earlier generations in the 20th century, and more than one-fourth of all New Boomer children born in the 1980s and 1990s were counted in homes missing one or both parents. The cross-sectional nature of census counts means that even greater shares of children in each generation actually experienced missing parents at some time between birth and the end of childhood.

Number of Siblings

Each child's life chances depend in part on how many brothers and sisters share the home. Figure 3.3 presents a vertical bar for each generation of children under age ten, divided to show the share who lived

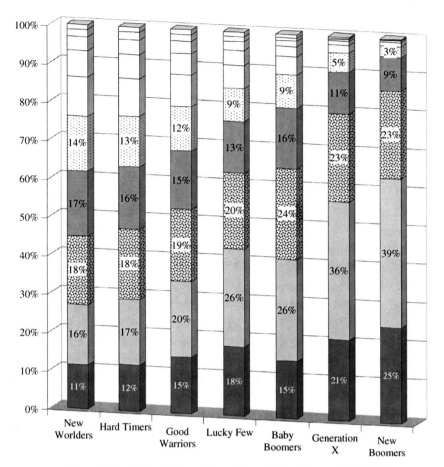

Fig. 3.3 Generations of children by number of siblings
Source: Original calculations from Census Public Use Microdata Samples.

with no siblings, one brother or sister, and so on at the time they were counted in different censuses.

As the twentieth century unfolded, American children lived with fewer and fewer brothers and sisters. At the beginning of the century a majority (55 percent) of young New Worlder children had at least three brothers and sisters in their homes. For the Lucky Few growing up in the middle of the century this share shrank to only about one-third of all young children, and by the end of the century less than one of every six New Boomer children lived with three or more siblings. Children in the largest families were counting each other as siblings (in other words, such families count once for each child), so the share of actual households with such large numbers of brothers and sisters shrinks away to almost nothing.

Instead of living in the midst of large families, more and more children were reported in each new census as the only child in the household, or perhaps living with one or two siblings. Even the Baby Boom could not reverse this trend entirely. Baby Boomer children indeed were less likely to be "only children" than were Good Warrior or Lucky Few children, but their homes instead had one or two other children present—not large families. The share of Baby Boomers living in large families actually fell below the share for the Lucky Few. The Baby Boom formed many new small families, rather than just making existing families larger.

What has this meant for children? The disappearance of brothers and sisters may have freed up more family resources for each child. If so, Lucky Few children were better off in that regard than children in previous generations, but not so lucky as the generations that came after them. In particular, more of the Lucky Few children grew up with *no* brothers or sisters than for any other generation until the two newest groups at the end of the century. Lucky Few children were more likely to be counted as the only child in the home while under age ten than were either the Good Warriors before them or the Baby Boomers after them. Some of the better-known "only children" among the Lucky few include former New York City mayor Rudy Giuliani, actor Robert DeNiro, singer Bobby Vinton and basketball coach Bobby Knight.

Folk wisdom used to hold that "the only child was the lonely child," that children without siblings often fell prey to various psychological problems, and that they grew into poorly-functioning adults because they had been spoiled by their parents. If these folk beliefs were true, the large number of only children among the Lucky Few would hardly count as part of their luck!

However, careful research (for example, see Blake 1989 and Falbo 1992) effectively discredits most of these old myths. Only children, similar in many ways to other first births, actually do well in school, possess high self-esteem, show no systematic disadvantages relating to peers, and also seem to have less trouble adopting adult roles once they grow up. They do not typically describe themselves as "lonelier" than do other children.

Ages of Parents

For children who did live with one or both parents, other facts about those parents could make big differences in the children's lives. For example, parents who are a little older than others when their children are born tend to be better-educated, to be more established in life, and to have more resources (both material and psychological) for dealing with the challenges of parenthood.

How old were the parents of the Lucky Few when these children were born, and how do those ages compare to parents of other generations? Whether each generation of children grows up with older or younger parents depends on two very different dynamics: different family sizes, and earlier or later ages of parents when they have their first birth.

If every mother bore her first child at the same age, later children born into larger families always would have older mothers. Baby Boomer George W. Bush was the first child born to his mother Barbara Bush. She was 21 years old in 1946 when she gave birth to the future President. But Mrs. Bush, a member of the Good Warrior generation, went on to have six children. Her sixth child (daughter Dorothy) was born 13 years later when Mrs. Bush had reached age 34.

If a generation of women produce fewer large families than previous generations (all other things equal), their average age as mothers would be younger as a result. We already know from Fig. 3.3 that families included smaller average numbers of children over the course of the twentieth century. By itself, this shrinking family trend should have meant younger average ages of mothers and fathers for each successive generation, since each generation included fewer high-order (fifth, sixth, etc.) births, usually born to older parents.

For most of the century, average ages of parents did fall for each new generation of children, just as we would expect as a result of shrinking family size. In fact for the first half of the century, the average ages of mothers and fathers actually fell faster than expected from the shrinking family effect alone (see Fig. 3.4), because couples also got married and started families at younger and younger ages (see Chapter 4).

However, Fig. 3.4 also illustrates a new trend affected the timing of family formation after mid-century. As the huge generation of Baby Boomers emerged from their crowded high schools and college

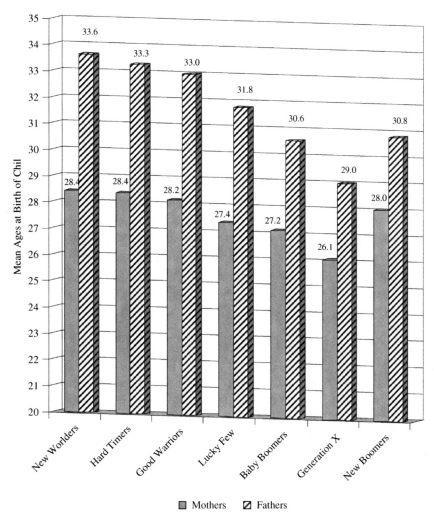

Fig. 3.4 Mean ages of parents by generation (all births)
Source: Original calculations from Census Public Use Microdata Samples.

campuses in the 1960s and encountered unexpected problems starting their careers, they married later. This also shifted first births to
older ages, a trend that only intensified for the rest of the century.
For example, Baby Boomer Hillary Clinton did not give birth to her
first and only daughter Chelsea until age 32, almost the same age as
Barbara Bush at the birth of her sixth child and more than a decade
older than Mrs. Bush had been at the time of her first son's birth.

George W. Bush's wife Laura did not give birth to her twin daughters Barbara and Jenna until after her 35th birthday.

These delays in family formation had a stronger effect on parental ages than the continued shrinking-family trend, first slowing and then reversing the shift toward younger parents. The final generation of the century, the New Boomers, actually had mothers whose older average age at birth matched that of the mothers of the Good Warrior generation born more than half a century earlier. The gap in age between mothers and fathers did continue to disappear across all generations, however, so that the fathers of the New Boomers were only as old, on average, as the fathers of the Baby Boom two generations earlier. Generation X children had the youngest parents of the twentieth century, with fathers who averaged 29 years old and mothers who averaged 26 years old when these children were born. (This average age applies not only to first births, but to *all* children in the generation.)

Studies of Childhood Stress

One of the most insightful descriptions of the consequences of living through the hardships of the 1930s comes from Glen Elder's unique book, *Children of the Great Depression* (1968). Elder used the unparalleled richness of observations from a longitudinal study that began with annual birth cohorts of 1920 and 1921 (right in the middle of the Good Warrior generation) as they attended school in Oakland, California. They were followed up with repeated interviews for the next half-century. From this continuous record of experience, Elder concluded that the temporary shock of unemployment, family disruption and the resulting emotional turmoil and confusion actually stimulated the coping skills of this generation, particularly the young people who experienced serious sudden deprivations but who had enjoyed a good standard of living before the crash.

Elder contrasted this stimulating result with the cynicism, defeatism and passivity that can emerge in a social context of prolonged, endemic poverty that spans multiple generations. The Great Depression was something more like a muscle spasm in the sinews of society, not a tissue-destroying abscess. Boys who saw their fathers' careers in ruins shifted some of their choices for role models to other figures outside the family, suggested Elder. (In his book "children" actually means "boys" since he didn't study any girls.) They looked more to their mothers for advice and guidance as well. But in many cases, they also saw their fathers fight their way back into the economy again as the economic spasm passed in the late 1930s. In their formative years, the Good Warriors came face to face with the harsh economic realities of life and learned to rely first of all upon themselves to cope with the challenge.

Many of these same psychological dynamics would apply with equal force to the Lucky Few children born during those times. They would have been younger than the Good Warriors featured in Elder's book, but they also would have seen parents lose jobs, and in many cases regain them again after some possibly desperate years. One old saying has it that "whatever doesn't kill you makes you stronger," and in the case of the Lucky Few, this might just be a useful way to sum up the impact of those early years on their later lives.

Rise of Mass Education

Home and family form most of the social environment for children during their earliest years. As they grow older, however, children in every generation come into more contact with the larger society outside the family home. In the United States in the twentieth century, going to school grew in importance as the first major step taken by children beyond their family households. In fact, the formalization of "schooling" as the dominant activity of childhood and adolescence took place between 1900 and 2000, and the Lucky Few found themselves at center-stage in this radical change in the way Americans grow up.

Most Americans had very limited experience with formal education at the dawn of the twentieth century. In colonial America and in the period immediately after independence, formal education beyond the simplest training in elementary skills of reading and writing only featured in the lives of a small elite of children whose parents had money, professional occupations, and/or privileged positions in society. In the late 1800s, as American cities and industry grew at a phenomenal pace, widespread formal public education first took root in these urban places. Even by 1900, though, one could hardly describe school attendance as "mass education." One of every ten adult men and one of every 12 adult women remained completely illiterate. Of all children between ages six and 18 counted in the 1880 census, only about half (54 percent) actually attended school. For the average person who thinks of almost all children attending school at ages six or seven, it may come as a surprise to learn that the share of children in school actually peaked at age eleven in every U.S. Census for most of the twentieth century, as demonstrated in Fig. 3.5.

The peak enrolments at age eleven in all these census counts resulted from a combination of two features of children's school experiences, both of which largely disappeared by the end of the century (along with the peak at age eleven). First, students used to leave school at earlier ages, so enrolment rates in the first decades of the century dropped fast after age eleven. Second, many children started school late and attended episodically, taking a season or even a year or two off in the middle of their school years as family circumstances required.

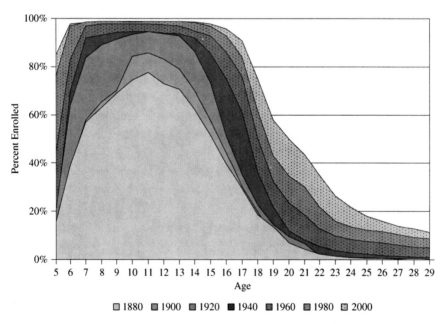

Fig. 3.5 School enrollment by age and year
Source: Original calculations from Census Public Use Microdata Samples.

This now-and-then attendance pattern appeared most frequently in rural areas, but also could be found in the new and growing cities, particularly among children living and working in factory districts. By age eleven or twelve some students had only progressed through the first few elementary grades, learning to read and write and perhaps to do some basic arithmetic. For many of them school came to an end at that point.

The first decades of the new century witnessed a leap forward in enrolments. By 1920 already three of every four children ages 6–18 attended school, spurred by two major changes in law and policy after 1900. The first change outlawed child labor in industry (Lovejoy 1911, Walters & Briggs 1993), removing the earlier incentive for families to put children to work rather than keeping them in school. The second change made school attendance compulsory up to some minimum age (Richardson 1980, Walters & Briggs 1993). Migration from farms to cities further reinforced the impact of these laws, which primarily affected urban families. By 1960 another forty years of expansion for schooling brought enrolment up to 90 percent of all potential students in these ages, leaving room for only slight further increases over the last four decades of the century.

Of course, with such intermittent schooling for young children, calendar age matched grade levels less closely than for children today. Studies from the 1940 census (Folger & Nam, 1967) showed that even close to the middle of the century, a third of all students were "too old" (by today's standard) for the grades they were attending, sometimes by several years. In 1880 or 1900 this variability must have been even greater. Today, though, we think more in terms of "correct" ages for grade levels, and age-for-grade has become more regimented.

Educational Backgrounds of Adult Generations

To see how the evolution of formal schooling translated into different educational results for successive generations, we look ahead for a moment at each generation in middle adulthood. More than eight of every ten New Worlders, already at ages 51–70 in the 1940 Census, reported that they had never finished high school. (The Census recorded detailed education for adults in the United States for the first time only in 1940, so we have no comparable information for earlier decades.)[1]

W also capture educational attainment of the Hard Timers in the 1940 Census at younger ages from 32 to 51. For younger generations we adopt the same age range as for Hard Timers, selecting a year when the youngest of them had reached age 32 (after education is virtually complete). These years were 1960 for the Good Warriors, 1977 for the Lucky Few, 1996 for the Baby Boomers, and 2007 for Generation X (the latter three documented using Current Population Surveys rather than decennial censuses). The most recent available figures for 2007 only found Generation X at ages 24–42, and so may understate their eventual share of college graduates. However, even by 2007 Generation X already had surpassed the Baby Boomers, setting new records for the largest share of college graduates among both men and women.

By midlife, as already noted, over eighty percent of New Worlders had left school without finishing the 12th grade. Only about one in twenty had finished college. Hard Timers only went a little further in school. Fully three-fourths of them never finished high school, and very few of them graduated from college. These outcomes come as no surprise given the low levels of enrolment noted during their childhood years. The Good Warrior generation made the first big jump toward mass education, with about half of them completing high school and also a noticeably larger share than for earlier generations graduating from college.

A larger percentage of women than men in every generation completed high school, except that Lucky Few women dropped out just as often as men. Men who did finish high school, on the other hand, then graduated from college much more often than women. In every generation up to Generation X, men usually had both more high school dropouts and more college graduates, while women concentrated more in the middle category of high school graduates without college diplomas (but see Chapter 8 for a different pattern among black Americans in all generations). Only in Generation X do we see women graduating from college more than men for the first time, as well as finishing high school more often.

If the Good Warriors made the first big step forward in mass education (half of the entire generation graduating from high school),

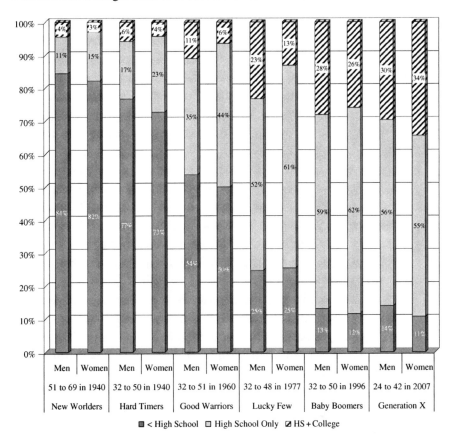

Fig. 3.6 Completed education for generations
Source: Original calculations from Census Public Use Microdata Samples.

Lucky Few men promptly outdid their achievement with the largest schooling improvement of the century. More than three-fourths of all Lucky Few men finished high school, and a full one-fourth of them graduated from college—more than double the share of male college graduates in the Good Warrior generation.

This phenomenal leap in college completion for the Lucky Few men, however, also produced another distinctive feature of their generation, because Lucky Few women did not participate as fully in this educational leap. For example, astronaut Neil Armstrong met his wife Janet while both were attending Purdue University. Neil went on to complete his undergraduate degree though he took time out to serve in Korea as a Navy pilot, and even went on to graduate studies, but Janet never finished her degree and regretted that fact later in her life. Among the Lucky Few, women matched men in the share failing to complete high school and lagged far behind the men in college attendance and graduation. Lucky Few women like Sandra Day O'Connor or Ruth Bader Ginsberg, the first two female justices ever appointed to the U.S. Supreme Court, were exceptions to this general rule of smaller education gains among the Lucky Few women.

In fact, the deficit in college education among Lucky Few women compared to men surpassed that of any other generation during the twentieth century. Earlier generations had less education, so naturally the gap between men and women was much smaller. But both the Baby Boomers and Generation X, who got even more education than the Lucky Few, also registered a more equal pattern of college attendance for men and women.

The education gap by sex for the Lucky Few provides a first glimpse of a recurrent pattern that we encounter in many other forms in later chapters. Lagging education for women forms one facet of a sharp division of roles by sex, a pattern that by the end of the century had become enshrined as "traditional" sex roles for men and women. We will examine just how traditional this sharp division of sex roles really has been in Chapters 4 and 6 below, when we come to the subject of work and careers.

In closing the present chapter about growing up, the figures on educational attainment furnish a conclusive final word on the long-term impact of difficulties in early life for the Lucky Few. These Americans came into the world during some of the most trying years of the twentieth century. Massive numbers of their fathers and mothers lost jobs, homes and other basics that most generations take for granted. In fact, times were so tough that many adults avoided parenthood altogether during these years, producing a smaller generation than those either before or after them. But Lucky Few children still enjoyed a high level of two-parent families during childhood, and by the time they reached high school and college, conditions had improved so much that Lucky Few men made the single biggest leap forward in mass education of any generation in the century. This small generation already had begun to experience the singular good fortune that would become the hallmark of their entire lives.

Note

1. Since more educated people live longer, educational attainment among
   survivors to older ages might actually *overstate* the average level of
   schooling for New Worlders reported in 1940. We can see how much difference twenty years of aging and mortality make for reported educational
   levels by looking at Hard Timers in 1940 and again in 1960, when they
   reach the older ages previously attained by New Worlders in 1940. As
   it turns out, the share of Hard Timer high school dropouts only changes
   from about 77 percent to 76 percent among these men after two decades
   of selective mortality. The educational distribution did "improve" because
   more of the least-educated men died, but the actual impact was trivial. We
   can include New Worlders in the figure despite their advanced ages by
   1940 when we finally find some information about their schooling.

Chapter 4
Growing Up Golden

Contents

Unfolding choices steer each of us down different life paths as we grow up. For people in the United States in the past century, these paths varied by generation as well as depending on many other features of people's backgrounds. For example, Chapter 3 showed that different generations had very different experiences with schooling. Each generation got more formal education than the generation before them, with Lucky Few men making the largest leap forward in schooling of any group in the twentieth century.

This chapter connects those decisions about school with the next major steps that people take out into society – the quest for a job, choosing whether and when to marry, and perhaps deciding the timing of a first birth and parenthood of the next generation.

Employment Versus Unemployment

Among scholars who study jobs in detail, many technical terms quickly make this subject very complex. We find references to the working ages, the civilian labor force, the employed population, and perhaps most peculiar of all, the concept of "unemployment." Contrary to what most people might expect, unemployment does not mean simply the absence of paid work. Many people such as students without jobs, homemakers, or disabled people unable to work are *not* technically unemployed as the government defines that term. In fact they are not in the labor force at all. The labor force includes only people working for pay or seeking paid employment. If you are not actively looking for a job, you don't count as either employed or unemployed – you fall outside the labor force entirely. Because "unemployment" rates leave an important fraction of people out of the picture, we avoid the term. Instead we look at employment itself. In this chapter, statistics giving percentages employed do not refer to employed persons as a share only of the labor force, but rather of the total population, avoiding the peculiarities afflicting the formal meaning of "unemployment."

Jobs for Generations

Figure 4.1 shows the percent of all men in each generation who reported being employed at various ages. Figures come from computerized public use samples (*http://cps.ipums.org/cps/*) of the annual Current Population Survey (CPS), available for all years since 1962. Ages shown at the bottom of the figure refer to the median members of each generation. For example, since the Lucky Few were born from 1929 to 1945, the median or middle birth year for that generation was 1937. Eight years of Lucky Few births came before 1937, and eight more years of Lucky Few births followed.

For the oldest (Hard Timer) and youngest (Generation X) generations shown in the figure, CPS data provide only a glimpse of the final or beginning years of men's working lives, but fortunately almost the entire career lifetimes of the Lucky Few fall within this period. The first available CPS data from 1962 captured the middle birth cohort of the Lucky Few at age 25, when the generation as a whole occupied ages 17–33. The final survey used here, from 2003, showed the middle birth cohort at age 66 when the generation ranged in ages from 58 to 74.

The left side of Fig. 4.1 shows that Lucky Few men enjoyed better early success in finding and keeping jobs than any other generation of the century. Their peak level of employment came when their middle 1937 birth cohort reached age 32 – the year 1969 (born in 1937 plus 32 years old). Nearly 95 percent of all Lucky Few men held paying jobs in 1969 when they were centered on this age. By contrast, when

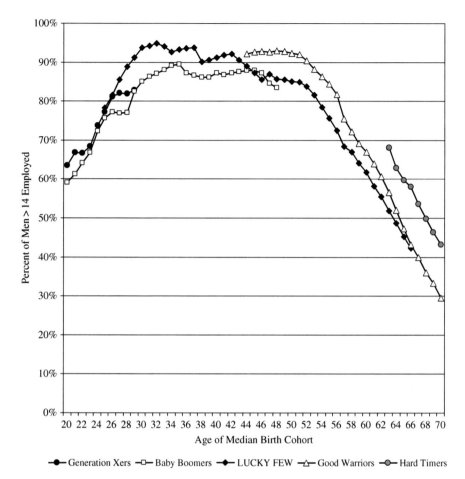

Fig. 4.1 Male employment by generation
Source: Original calculations from Current Population Survey Public Use
Microdata Samples.

the median Generation X or Baby Boomer men reached their early
thirties only about 85 percent held paying jobs. Even in their peak
employment year of 1990, Baby Boomer men failed to reach 90 percent employed. Compared to the fully-employed Lucky Few, nearly
twice as big a share of these young men lacked paying jobs at peak
employment ages.

The level of employment for Lucky Few men dipped slightly to
a plateau around 90 percent as this generation moved through their
forties and into their fifties, and then declined steadily to only about 45

percent employed when their median members reached age 65. (See the right side of Fig. 4.1). This makes sense because by that point, over half the generation were older than normal retirement ages while the rest were still in their late fifties or early sixties.

Although employment rates for men did vary from one generation to the next, the general age profile of paid work for men remained basically similar throughout the twentieth century. The most interesting feature of the right side of Fig. 4.1 shows that earlier generations stayed at work longer than the Lucky Few. For example, in 1964 when the middle Hard Timer men were 65 years old, almost two-thirds of that generation were still employed, compared to less than half (45 percent) of the Lucky Few centered on age 65 two generations later. Hard Timer men did not drop as low as 45 percent employed until they reached an average age of nearly 70. Each new generation of men has been withdrawing from paid employment at earlier ages, despite the fact (discussed in Chapter 9) that people in each generation also live longer and spend more of their lives in better health.

For women, the century brought nothing short of a revolution in terms of jobs. Valerie K. Oppenheimer (1982) spotted the early-life career struggles noted above for the Baby Boom men, and in fact attributed part of the wider paid employment for Baby Boom women as compensating for the job problems encountered by the men in their generation. Just as she suggested, Fig. 4.2 below for women looks very different from the picture for men. Though each new generation of men began withdrawing from employment earlier than the generation before them, women produced the opposite trend. Reaching higher levels of employment in middle adulthood, each new generation of women stayed at work longer than the generation before them. The later working lives of men and women grew more similar in each successive generation as employment rates converged. (We should remember, though, that official employment figures overstate this increase for women because early in the century many couples lived and worked on farms. While male farmers counted in the labor force, their farm wives were not included even though they worked just as hard.)

Early twentieth-century generations of women, challenged to combine motherhood with paid employment, tended to sequence these activities rather than trying to combine them. They stayed at home with children in early adulthood, then often went to work later in life.

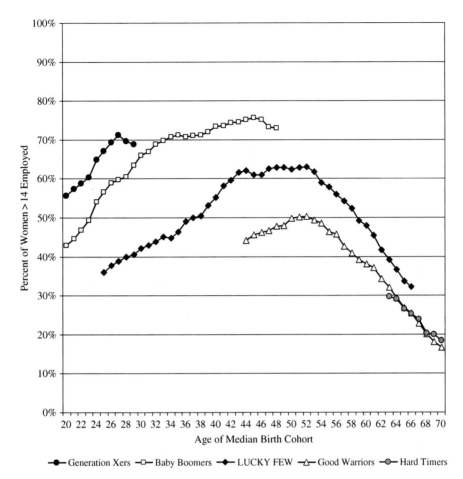

Fig. 4.2 Female employment by generation
Source: Original calculations from Current Population Survey Public Use
Microdata Samples.

As a consequence, women tended to reach their peak years of paid
employment much later in life than did men. Women in the Good
Warrior generation reached a peak of 50 percent employed at median
age 52 in 1970. By comparison, Lucky Few women reached a higher
peak of 63 percent employed in 1989, also at median age 52. This
looks like an impressive gain in jobs for women, until we observe that
the Baby Boom women then reached a peak of 75 percent employed,
and reached this peak almost a decade earlier in their lives, when the
median Baby Boomer woman was only 45 years old (that is, in 1998).

Each generation of women thus began employment earlier in life and rose more rapidly to a higher peak level than previous generations. Part of this pattern is due to the fact, explored below, that women had fewer children. Employment rates for women in our earliest generations peaked only after children were old enough for mothers to work outside the home. Earlier and more widespread employment for women in later generations reflected not only smaller families and so an earlier "empty nest," but also more working mothers of younger and younger children.

Valerie Oppenheimer in an earlier journal article (1967) and book (1970) provided an excellent picture of how expanding demand for female labor during most of the twentieth century gradually drew more women into paying jobs. First many Good Warrior mothers with grown children were drawn into the work force in the economic boom of the late 1950s, leaving most mothers of smaller children still at home. This helps to explain their generation's median age of 52 at peak employment rates. When the Lucky Few generation reached the middle working ages, the small size of their generation sharpened the labor shortage of both men and women. There simply were not enough women with grown children to satisfy the demand for workers, and nearly all the Lucky Few men also already were working. This combination of rapid economic growth and small numbers of young adult workers in the 1960s and 1970s drew in not only Lucky Few women with grown children but also mothers of children still in school. "Latch-key" Baby Boomer children came home from school, used a key to get into the house, and waited for their Lucky Few parents to come home from work.

This trend toward more paid employment for mothers of ever younger children has persisted down to the present. When Baby Boom women became mothers themselves, for example, even mothers of the youngest children often sought jobs. Their employment created the modern day-care industry in the United States. Generation X women, though they have barely begun their working careers, so far are running ahead of Baby Boomers in their early and widespread entry into paying jobs (but see Vere 2007 for possible heterogeneity within Generation X itself on this point).

Scholars continue to debate both sides of the motivational coin that stimulated entry into the labor force by mothers of even the very youngest children – was it based on the necessity of going to work

for the rising share of single mothers (see below) and women whose
Baby Boomer husbands experienced difficult career starts? Or was it
based on new opportunities created by rising education of women and
by campaigns for greater women's rights? Both explanations probably
have merit.

High Tide for Marriages

Demographers like to point out that both stand-up comedy and vital events are all about timing. In any generation, everyone starts out
unmarried at birth. Eventually over ninety percent of women in every generation have married. (We consider only the fact of ever having married here – the question of marital dissolution through death
or divorce comes up in later chapters.) New Worlder women early
in the century registered the smallest share ever marrying (about 92
percent of all women). As might be expected, Lucky Few women
take the prize for the most-married generation (about 95 percent of
all women ever married) but this contrast between the most-married
and least-married generations really doesn't amount to a very big
difference.

The real story involves how differently the generations have managed the timing of this shift from everyone single to virtually everyone
married. Tremendous variation appears in marriage timing. For con-
sistency, this chapter adopts the same approach used for children in the
previous chapter. Again we examine everyone in a specific ten-year
age range, capturing each generation in several adjacent censuses.
This strategy allows us to count everyone in each generation exactly
one time, and to consider each generation in the same age range.

To capture dramatic differences and trends in marriage timing seen
during the twentieth century, we examine a ten-year range from ages
20 to 29. In fact, while early and late marriages always occur, the majority of first marriages take place in every modern American generation in a narrow range between roughly ages twenty and thirty years
old. Figure 4.3 shows the percentage of women in each generation
who had ever married at each age from 20 to 29, the heart of the
marrying ages.

Only six of our seven generations appear in Fig. 4.3, because most
New Boomers born at the end of the century have not lived through

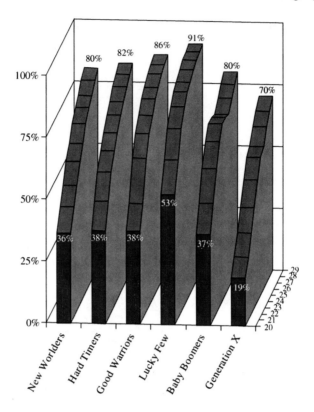

■ New Worlders ■ Hard Timers ■ Good Warriors ■ Lucky Few ■ Baby Boomers ■ Generation X

Fig. 4.3 Percent of women ever married (ages 20–29)
Source: Original calculations from Census Public Use Microdata Samples.

this age range between twenty and thirty. It remains to be seen how many of them will have married at each age. Still, these six generations give us a very clear picture of generational contrasts in marriage timing.

Lucky Few women, starting down their unparalleled paths of success in life, optimistically got married earlier and in greater numbers than any other generation in American history. The other "outlier" generation, Generation X, reveals an opposite tendency of much less marriage at each age than for other generations. Figure 4.4 shows the same leading position for Lucky Few men and the same trailing contrast for Generation X men. Since men marry later than women in all generations, the overall percentages ever married during their twenties

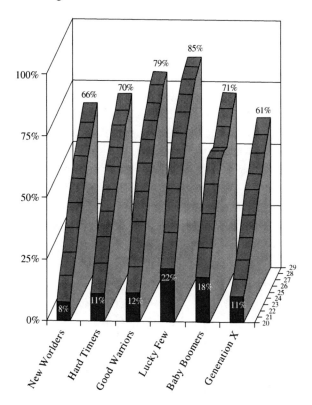

■ New Worlders ■ Hard Timers ■ Good Warriors ■ Lucky Few ■ Baby Boomers ■ Generation X

Fig. 4.4 Percent of men ever married (ages 20–29)
Source: Original calculations from Census Public Use Microdata Samples.

are lower for men than for women, but the generational contrasts are the same for both sexes. For both men and women, the Good Warriors and Hard Timers (older than the Lucky Few) and the Baby Boomers (younger than the Lucky Few) entered marriage at a slower pace, and Generation X falls far behind even these other slower generations.

This optimistic rush into marriage by the Lucky Few actually makes a strange combination with one of the main points of the preceding chapter – the great leap in more formal schooling made by this same generation. Ordinarily, people who go to school longer also marry later. Most people don't marry while still in school, or they leave school when they decide to get married – cause and effect can run in either direction. Yet as we have just seen, the Lucky Few men, who advanced much further in school than earlier generations, also married *earlier* than any other generation in the history of the United States. How did they manage to combine more school with earlier marriage?

Because Americans expect married couples to form their own independent households, historically there has been a time lag between the end of schooling and formation of marriages. Both events tend to cluster around a central or normal age, so we look at the time interval or "window" between the median age at leaving school and the median age at first marriage, as shown in Fig. 4.5a,b.

For example, in 1900 half of all men and women had stopped going to school by age 15. Yet in that year half of all men still remained unmarried at age 25, so for men the "window" between leaving school and entering marriage averaged about ten years wide. Women were almost 23 before half of them had gotten married, leaving a window

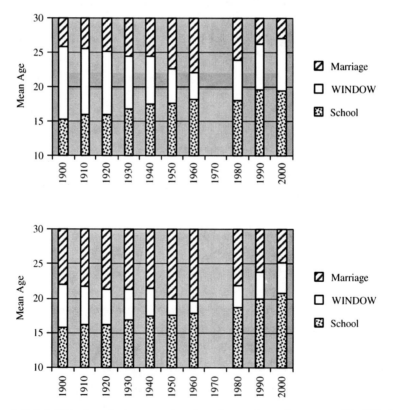

Fig. 4.5 **(a)** Window between school and marriage for men; **(b)** Window between school and marriage for women

Source: Original calculations from Census Public Use Microdata Samples.

of eight years on average between school and marriage. During the intervening ages, men tried to get established in careers, often seeking to inherit, homestead or purchase land for farms. Their potential wives had to wait, and also had to accumulate their dowries or trousseaus.

For each new generation prior to the Lucky Few, this window between finishing school and getting married gradually narrowed. The bottom of the window closed upward as people stayed in school longer. The top of the window also closed downward as people married earlier in each generation.

Paying jobs, the first topic considered in this chapter, actually explain much the apparent paradox of more schooling but earlier marriage for the Lucky Few. Earlier generations married at older ages because it took them longer to get established in life – to reach the point when a couple could survive independently. Steady improvements in the standard of living in the United States meant that each generation found it easier than their predecessors to achieve the economic stability needed for couples to marry and establish separate new households. We already have seen in this chapter that more of the Lucky Few men got jobs earlier in life than for any other generation. This small generation in the right place at the right time therefore found it easier to get married than any other generation. In fact, Fig. 4.5 shows that the window between leaving school and entering marriage practically closed altogether, at least for Lucky Few women.

Since that time, though, the window has begun to open again. While Baby Boomers got even more formal schooling than the Lucky Few, they also delayed their marriages much more. The gap between leaving school and getting married began to widen again, and has continued to widen for Generation X. Eventually we will be able to see whether this trend also continues for the New Boomers born at the close of the century.

Taken together, these mutually reinforcing trends produced two generations (to some extent, the Good Warriors later in their lives as well as the Lucky Few from their earliest adult years) who actually led atypical lives. When we consider the combined trends in formal schooling, starting jobs and getting married, each separate aspect of the transition to adulthood emphasizes the unparalleled good fortune of the Lucky Few generation. The sharp differentiation of gender roles for men and women in those years meant that generational success in the "public" sphere of schooling and jobs mainly accrued to men, while generational success found expression among Lucky Few women predominantly in the "private" sphere of family life. Another manifestation of this same success for women mainly in the private sphere of the home concerns generational differences in childbearing.

Motherhood Mania and the Baby Boom

The final feature of the life course considered in this chapter fits naturally with the previous look at starting jobs and getting married. At the same time that the Lucky Few and our other generations made marriage and job decisions, they also were deciding about having children. It should come as no surprise by now that Lucky Few women (and some of the younger Good Warrior women) became the mothers of the Baby Boom. After all, we have just seen that they married earlier and in greater numbers than any other generation. Another hint could come from observations in the previous chapter: Lucky Few women lagged behind Lucky Few men in formal schooling by a wider margin than was true for women in other generations. The children they bore constitute one reason for this.

The Baby Boom has been studied in great detail already (Easterlin 1961, Smith & Welch 1981, Lewis & Ha 1988) so we will not explore the wave of births themselves much here, beyond what has been said already in Chapters 2 and 3. Instead, we focus more on the mothers of the Baby Boom generation, with particular attention to the Lucky Few since they were at the heart of it. We consider three aspects of childbearing in successive generations: the timing of the first birth, the share of all women in each generation who remained childless through the end of the reproductive ages, and the numbers of children mothers had by the time they completed childbearing.

Just as Fig. 4.3 showed most of the marriages formed in each generation, Fig. 4.6 below shows the transition into motherhood for most Good Warrior, Lucky Few and Baby Boomer women. (Since the census did not ask the number of children ever born to women in the 1920 or 1930 censuses, we cannot include earlier generations like the Hard Timers. Since the youngest member of Generation X only reached age 18 by 2000, we cannot include younger generations, either.)

Fig. 4.6 Percent of
women with births
(ages 20–29)
Source: Original
calculations from
Census Public Use
Microdata Samples.

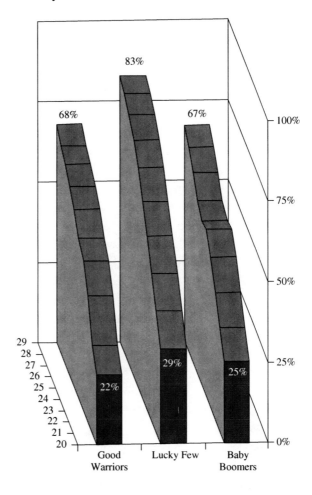

This Figure highlights once again the exceptional character of the
Lucky Few generation. They began having babies earlier than either
the Good Warriors before them or the Baby Boomers who followed
them. In fact, almost one-third of all Lucky Few women already had a
first child by age 20, compared to only about one-fifth of Good Warrior or Baby Boomer women. The Lucky Few maintained this lead at
every age during the third decade of their lives. By age 25 over two-
thirds of Lucky Few women had become mothers, while only half of
the women in the Good Warrior or Baby Boom generations had taken
this step. Birth statistics for even older or younger generations would
make the uniqueness of the Lucky Few stand out even more sharply.
Generation X women have delayed their first births even more than

the Baby Boomers. From what we do know about the Hard Timers'
lives, we may guess that they also delayed their births just as they
delayed their marriages.

The share of all women becoming mothers rises rapidly between
ages 20 and 29, as shown in Fig. 4.6 above, but some women in
every generation remain childless all their lives. Just as the Lucky
Few women rushed optimistically into marriage and parenthood earlier than other generations of the century, the other side of this coin
meant that the share of Lucky Few women remaining permanently
childless shrank to historic low levels.

Figure 4.6 above does not reach far enough into life to give us
conclusive evidence on this point. We need to consider childlessness among women in each generation when they have reached ages
where few further births can change the share never becoming mothers. Therefore we again look ahead in life, to consider women at ages
from 40 to 49. Only a tiny number of women without births by these
ages ever bear a child before menopause, so we may take the share of
mothers at these ages as very close to the final figure for each generation.

Fully 25 percent of Hard Timer women observed in their forties in
1940 or 1950 remained childless as they approached the end of their
childbearing years. In many cases these childless women also had
never married. When thinking about childlessness in each of our seven
generations of Americans, remember that in earlier decades nearly all
childlessness was involuntary (Poston & Gotard 1977). A higher level
of childlessness among the Hard Timers provides stark confirmation
of the many hardships and limitations experienced by that generation
in the early decades of the century.

The Good Warrior women who followed them (observed in their
forties across the 1950, 1960 or 1970 censuses) give equally clear
evidence that despite the interruptions of wartime, their generation
experienced more opportunities than the Hard Timers. Only 15 percent of all Good Warrior women remained childless by the time they
were in their forties.

But as usual, the demographic prize again goes to the Lucky Few.
Barely eleven percent of women in the Lucky Few remained childless
by the time they reached their forties (counted in the censuses of 1970,
1980 or 1990). The previous section showed that the share of women

never marrying among the Lucky Few shrank to less than half the share observed among most other generations during the century. Here we add that the share never having a child also fell by half in comparison to other generations. Not only did the Lucky Few women begin marrying and having children earlier in life – they also continued this high tide of family formation until it had swept a larger share of their number into marriage and motherhood than for any other generation of the century.

The Baby Boom women who followed the Lucky Few reverted to the higher level of childlessness seen for earlier generations. Not only did Baby Boom women stay in school longer, marry later, and start careers more often (all of which affected their options, attitudes and decisions about children) but even those women who eventually decided to have children sometimes encountered physiological limits that increase with age, contributing to that higher level of childlessness. So far, women in Generation X are remaining childless in even greater numbers than for the Baby Boom generation.

We already considered the final aspect of childbearing, number of births, from the viewpoint of children (see the previous chapter). Here we reverse the binoculars and view the same patterns from the viewpoint of the parents. The total number of children born to each generation results from a combination of two things: first, the share of women who become mothers (discussed above) and second, the average number of children born to those mothers. Figure 4.7 reveals both the long-term downward trend in average family size for mothers during the twentieth century, and once again, the exceptional situation of the Lucky Few generation.

With the exception of the Lucky Few, each generation of mothers had smaller average family sizes than the generation before them. While New Worlder mothers averaged nearly four children each (some having only one, but some having many more), mothers born during the Baby Boom experienced such a different world that they averaged less than three births each. Only the Lucky Few stand out from this long-term decline in family size. Lucky Few mothers actually averaged more children than the Great Warrior generation before them. However, it is interesting to see in this Figure that the fruitfulness of Lucky Few mothers only brought them back up to the level of the Hard Timer mothers. Set against the backdrop of the century-long

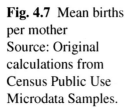

Fig. 4.7 Mean births per mother
Source: Original calculations from Census Public Use Microdata Samples.

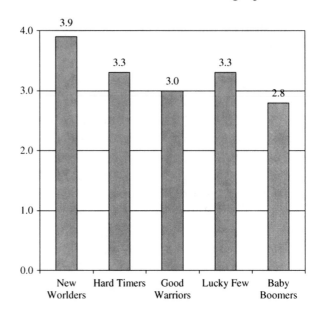

decline in average family size, this temporary increase for the Lucky Few mothers is significant but should be kept in perspective for the short-term fluctuation that it really was.

In this chapter we examined the exceptional lives of the Lucky Few from several important angles as they advanced from childhood into adult roles including jobs, marriage and parenthood. Several important facts stand out from this examination. First, the men in the Lucky Few came closer to complete full employment than any other generation, and apparently prospered so well that they began retiring considerably earlier than previous generations. Second, Lucky Few women did participate in the rising tide of paid employment seen for each new generation of women during the century, but a sharp division of sex roles for men and women meant that "success" for the Lucky Few appeared more for men in the public sphere of education and jobs, and more for women in the private sphere of home and family. Third, the Lucky Few married much earlier than any other generation despite their gains in formal schooling, and so "closed the window" between school and marriage more than for any other generation. Fourth, men's career success led the Lucky Few into early marriages and made them parents of the Baby Boom, having more children earlier than other generations, reducing childlessness to historic low levels, and temporarily reversing the century-long decline in average family size among mothers.

Considering all the generations of the twentieth century, many of the patterns observed after the Lucky Few among Baby Boomers and Generation X suggest a return to patterns observed in the first two generations of the century – the New Worlders and the Hard Timers. In time, history may well show us that the Good Warrior and Lucky Few generations, whose experiences today often define "traditional" or "normal" family and work roles, in fact represented an unusual temporary detour from quite different patterns of life for most other generations in American society – a fascinating paradox in the making.

The next chapter devotes special attention to yet another feature of these young adult years of life – a feature that sets the Lucky Few apart even more sharply than the patterns examined in this or the previous chapter. We turn now to the military service experience of each of our twentieth-century generations of Americans.

Chapter 5
Peacetime Patriots

Contents

A Century of Military Service

We know from previous chapters that the societal trauma of war can have powerful, permanent effects on generations and their perceptions of themselves. To see how and to what extent each of our generations participated in various conflicts, this chapter examines the evolution of military service over the twentieth century. In Fig. 5.1 showing U.S. active-duty military personnel by age during the twentieth century, the period after 1945 stands out clearly as different from the first half of the century. Prior to mid-century, peacetime always meant demobilization of military forces. After the Civil War, the Spanish-American War or the First World War, only a tiny cadre of professional officers and career soldiers remained on duty. For example, the military forces of the United States totalled only about 135,000 men between

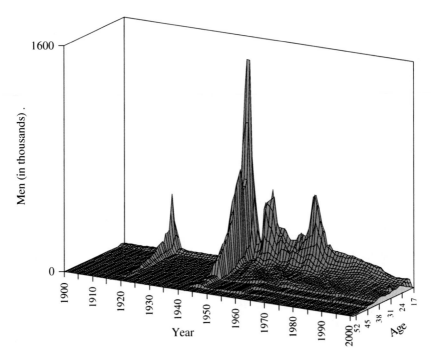

Fig. 5.1 U.S. men on active military duty by age and year (1900–2000)
Source: Statistical Abstract of the United States,
Historical Statistics of the United States,
Department of Defense. Selected Manpower Statistics (selected years).

1901 and 1916. Despite the sudden expansion to nearly three million
soldiers during the First World War in 1918, again by 1926 less than
250,000 personnel remained on active duty.

This "feast or famine" for the military establishment changed fundamentally in the second half of the century, when the size and budget
of the newly-established Department of Defense became a permanent
military "feast" at the table of the American economy. After the 1945
wartime peak in active-duty soldiers to over 12 million persons, the
post-war military did shrink again, but this time only to a minimum
of about 1.4 million people in uniform by 1948. The total returned
to over three million people on active duty during the Korean conflict,
and then *stayed* between 2.5 and 3 million for the next quarter-century
(except during Vietnam, when the total rose briefly to match the 3.5
million peak from the Korean era). Between 1946 and 1971, in effect the United States never demobilized at all (Segal & Segal 2004).

Active-duty forces always totalled more than *ten times* the size of the military between the two world wars. Only after Vietnam, with the advent of the all-volunteer armed force in the mid-1970s, did the active-duty population go into a long-term decline from the 2.5 million mark. This gradual decline continued to the end of the century, leaving only about one million people on active duty by the year 2000.

In terms of generations, at least some New Worlders fought in the Spanish-American War at the dawn of the twentieth century. The Hard Timer generation fought in the First World War. The classic case of a generation shaped by war, though, involves the Good Warriors – that generation who fought in the Second World War. Their voices and experiences have been captured for posterity in Tom Brokaw's book, *The Greatest Generation*. Brokaw himself was born in 1940, making him one of the Lucky Few who, as discussed below, were too young to fight in Korea. In any case Brokaw was not drafted and, like half the men in his generation, never served in the military. He progressed directly from college into broadcast journalism.

In the second half of the century the Lucky Few fought in Korea as young men, and in some cases again as senior officers or enlisted personnel in Vietnam. The Baby Boomers furnished the young draftees and volunteers serving at entry-level ranks in Vietnam. The members of Generation X formed the bulk of American combat forces in the Middle East, both in Operation Desert Storm in the 1990s and again in Afghanistan and Iraq during the first decade of the twenty-first century. A few of the oldest among the New Boomers reached the battlefield ages in time for the latter conflicts.

The Spanish-American War

Technically, of course, the Spanish-American War belongs to the nineteenth century rather than the twentieth. However, the generation occupying the battlefield ages during the war, the New Worlders born between 1871 and 1889, carried their experiences from that conflict through the rest of their lives during the twentieth century. We call the ages between 17 and 24 "battlefield ages" because military records show that at least during the twentieth century, most enlisted men were at these ages when they actually saw combat on the front lines in military conflicts. Their officers often were older, but older officers and senior enlisted men in career military service tend to find themselves more and more removed from the battlefield and the risk of violent death.

Following an explosion that sank the battleship *U.S.S. Maine* in the harbor of Havana, Cuba in the Spring of 1898, the United States fought a "summer war" that began when Spain declared war on April 24th. The war ended with Spain's surrender on August 22nd after a string of overwhelming American victories. After the cessation of hostilities the United States kept some New Worlders in uniform to help keep order in the empire of overseas holdings the country suddenly inherited from Spain, but on the whole New Worlders withdrew from military life after the war ended.

Twenty years later, when the youngest of the New Worlders already had celebrated his 29th birthday, some of these youngest members of the generation again found themselves caught up in war, serving as officers and senior enlisted men among the American doughboys who shipped out for Europe in 1917 to fight in the First World War. The size of the American military during that conflict was so much bigger than during the Spanish American War, in fact, that more New Worlders fought in the First World War than against Spain, though they amounted to only a small minority comprising the oldest members of the American forces in Europe.

Finally, a handful of New Worlder career soldiers were still on active duty at the outbreak of the Second World War. The youngest of them was already 52 years old when the Japanese attacked Pearl Harbor so their participation was demographically insignificant, but they included many of the top commanders in the war. For example, Admiral Edward Kimmel, the Commander in Chief of the Pacific who was relieved of duty following the surprise attack on Pearl Harbor, was a New Worlder born in 1882. So were the admirals who stayed on in the Pacific to win the war: Admiral Chester Nimitz (born 1885), Admiral William "Bull" Halsey (born 1882), Admiral Raymond Spruance (born 1886) and others. Similarly, leading generals such as George Patton (born 1885), Douglas MacArthur (born 1880) and George C. Marshall (also born 1880) belonged to the New Worlder generation. Marshall went on to become Secretary of State and Secretary of Defense, and to craft a postwar global strategy that bears his name: the Marshall Plan.

The First World War

Many New Worlders sailed to Europe after the United States declared war on Germany in late 1917, joining another new generation in the trenches in France as front-line combat soldiers in that first global conflict of the new century – the Hard Timers born from 1890 to 1908. New Worlders like the iconic Army Corporal Alvin York fought together with Hard Timers including flying ace Lieutenant Eddie Rickenbacker of the Army Air Corps, Army Private Thomas Neibaur and Marine Corps Corporal John Pruitt. All of these men received the Congressional Medal of Honor (Pruitt receiving both Army and Navy medals for the same action).

To gain a more systematic view of generational participation in this and other conflicts, we can view not just at the records of a few out-standing individuals but the service experience of entire generations as a whole. Since each birth cohort in each generation "ages" diagonally across the surface of Fig. 5.1 above, growing one year older with each passing calendar year, we can count person-years of military service by following such diagonals across the surface of the figure for each generation. Dividing the resulting total of person-years of service by the total number of person-years lived in each generation during the relevant age range (from 17 to 54) gives an "intensity" or "hazard" of military service. This service intensity appears in Fig. 5.2 below as

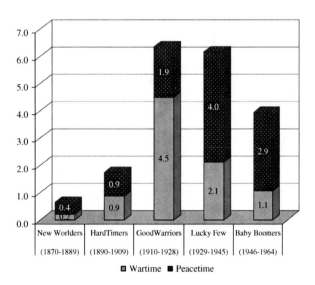

Fig. 5.2 Years of active duty per 100 person-years lived, (ages 17–54) Source: calculated from the data used for Fig. 5.1, combined with population estimates by age and year derived from decennial U.S. Census counts.

person-years served per 100 person-years lived between ages 17 and 54 by all the men in each generation.

This Figure shows what one might already suspect from the preceding discussion of the Spanish-American War. The New Worlder generation had a very low overall level of military service. Hard Timers, by virtue of occupying the battlefield ages during the First World War, experienced more extensive military involvement. However, at the end of that war most of them were demobilized and only the career soldiers among the Hard Timers were still in uniform by the outbreak of the Second World War – what we called in Chapter 2 the "Good War."

The Second World War

It is easy to see why the Good War left such an indelible stamp on the Good Warriors when we remember that about two-thirds of all men in that generation actually served in the military during wartime. No other American generation of the century even comes close to that scale of participation. One caveat: most discussion in this chapter centers on men in the military, but not out of any intention to slight the contributions of women. Although women serve today with distinction in the armed forces of the United States, such participation on a large scale began relatively recently, and attention to women in uniform by those who collect official statistics began even more recently. For example, the U.S. Census only began asking women about their veteran status in 1980, so we have no population-based information about such status for earlier decades.

Confirming the paramount impact of the Good Warriors and World War II, Fig. 5.1 shows the pronounced spike in military participation produced during the early 1940s by the wartime draft and a parallel surge of voluntary enlistments. Following these soldiers diagonally across that Figure and so forward through time, we arrive at a much higher intensity of lifetime military service for the Good Warriors than for either of the first two generations of the century – about ten times higher than for New Worlders and four times higher than for Hard Timers. Further, Fig. 5.2 shows that fully three-fourths of all military service by Good Warrior men took place during wartime – mostly during the Second World War, but also to some extent as leaders at senior ranks during Korea and even Vietnam. For example, General William

Westmoreland (a Good Warrior born in 1914 into a prosperous South Carolina family) fought in the Second World War, led a combat team in Korea, and capped his military career as the commander of American forces in Vietnam.

The Peacetime Military Establishment

The early years of the 1900s saw the unravelling of colonial empires constructed around the world during earlier centuries. In the second half of the century, however, a very different struggle obscured this colonial unravelling. The Cold War was based not on economics or *realpolitik* or the other concerns that had preoccupied pre-war imperial powers, but rather on an ideological contest. The Lucky Few generation and those that have followed them came of age in this Cold War epoch, when the global role of the United States had changed dramatically. Military accomplishments of the Good Warriors on battlefields around the world established the United States as the planet's leading superpower and the leader of the western bloc of nations in their confrontation with the Soviet Union, China, and the communist bloc. This fundamental shift to superpower status accounts for the striking difference between the first and second halves of the century in Fig. 5.1 above, and explains the resulting massive standing peacetime military establishment in the United States. The timing of this mid-century shift affected one generation above all – the Lucky Few.

The Korean Conflict

Although it never became an actual war declared by the Congress, the police action in Korea produced another crest (visible in Fig. 5.1 above) in the number of Americans serving on active duty in the armed forces. When the Korean conflict flared into open fighting involving U.S. troops in 1950, the oldest Lucky Few soldier (born in 1929) was only 21 years old and the youngest member of the generation was still in kindergarten. Still, this meant that 41 percent of the men on active military duty in 1950 belonged to the Lucky Few. By 1953, when the armistice divided Korea into North and South along the 38th parallel of latitude and halted the fighting, 72 percent of the men on active military duty and *all* of the men in the battlefield ages were Lucky Few soldiers.

Thus virtually all the Lucky Few winners of the Medal of Honor were clustered in the battlefield ages during the Korean conflict – men such as Army Private Luther Story of the Second Infantry Division, born in Buena Vista, Georgia in 1931 and killed in action at Agok, Korea in 1950; Marine Corps Private Eugene Obregon of the First Marine Division, born in Los Angeles in 1930 and killed in action near Seoul, Korea in 1950; Army Private Richard Wilson of the 82nd Airborne Infantry, born in Marion, Illinois in 1931 and killed in action at Opari, Korea in 1950; or Navy Hospital Corpsman Richard Dewart attached to the First Marine Division, born in 1931 in Taunton, Massachusetts and killed in action in Korea in 1952. This list of men who fought with valor and often died for their country could go on for many pages, but the point about the battlefield ages is clear.

Older active-duty troops in Korea included younger members of the Good Warriors, some of them veterans of the Second World War while others were too young to have fought in that conflict. These Good Warriors (and even some older officers from earlier generations) now found themselves in Korea, usually like William Westmoreland as officers and leaders of the Lucky Few. Some of the oldest Lucky Few men themselves also managed to serve as officers in Korea in exceptional cases – Lucky Few astronaut Neil Armstrong, who would later become the first man on the Moon, took time out from his college education at Purdue University to train as a Navy pilot in Pensacola. He served a tour of duty as a jet pilot in the Korean conflict, where he was shot down while flying a reconnaissance mission.

How did the Lucky Few's war compare to the wars of other generations? First of all, unlike all previous wars of the United States, the Lucky Few did not all go to Korea *en masse*. The country did not experience a sudden massive mobilization and departure of millions of troops all at once. For the first time, U.S. military strategists experimented with a new doctrine based on the new reality of a permanent standing peacetime military force. With young men reaching service ages and registering for the draft every year, military strategists introduced the rotation system. A smaller but steady stream of troops continuously cycled in and out of the conflict, serving their tours of duty and then returning to the United States. This rotation system, rather than any shift in public attitude or anything else, probably accounts for why the Korean conflict is sometimes called the "forgotten war." With no massive mobilization and departure of a huge army, and no sudden and equally massive return of such a vast force when the armistice was declared, the overwhelming mass rituals and celebrations that marked the start and end of the two World Wars earlier in the century simply never happened across America. We have no iconic photographs from the end of the Korean War, no picture to rival that famous sailor-kissing-the-nurse photo from New York City that captured the jubilant mood at the end of our Good War.

In 1950, at the outbreak of the Korean conflict, about 590,000 men from the Lucky Few were serving on active military duty, totalling about eleven percent of the Lucky Few male population in the same ages (17–21) of 5.4 million. By 1953, when Lucky Few men filled all the battlefield ages from 17 to 24 they contributed 2.5 million men in uniform, representing almost thirty percent of a total population in this age range of 8.5 million men. With soldiers rotating through the military and in and out of Korea, however, the cumulative percent of these men who became military veterans actually rose higher than these fractions on active duty at any particular date. In the 1960 census, for example, more than half of all these older Lucky Few men reported themselves as veterans of military service, as shown in Fig. 5.5 below.

On the other hand, most of the Lucky Few generation was too young for the Korean conflict. For enlisted men, only those born before 1934 were old enough for military service in Korea. Only officers born in 1929 or 1930, the very first birth cohorts of the Lucky Few, would have been likely to fight in Korea because officers typically graduated from college before going on active duty. Thus although H. Ross Perot was born in 1930 in Texarkana, Texas, he did not manage to graduate from the Naval Academy as a Lieutenant Junior-grade until 1953, too late for the Korean conflict. Eventually, of course, he left his civilian job at IBM to found Electronic Data Systems and make a fortune selling computers to the federal government, and then ran as a third-party candidate for President of the United States. All the rest of the Lucky Few born in later years were too young for Korea. This also appears clearly in census reports of veteran status. While over 60 percent of the older Lucky Few men report veteran status, only a little over one-third of the younger Lucky Few men reported that they were military veterans – the generation is not "homogenous" with regard to military service.

As with any war in the modern era of extremely complex military operations, even at the peak of the Korean conflict most U.S. soldiers even in the battlefield ages were not actually on the battlefield. In fact in 1952, when desperate battles with massive Chinese armies in Korea reached such deadly intensity that American leaders seriously began to consider using battlefield nuclear weapons, 90 percent of all U.S. armed forces were not in the Korean peninsula at all. Award-winning actor and director Clint Eastwood, born in 1930 in San Francisco, was among the oldest of the Lucky Few and eligible to fight in Korea when he was drafted into the Army in 1949, a year after finishing Oakland Technical High School. However, Eastwood spent the years of the Korean War as a swimming instructor at Fort Ord, near Monterey, California.

Figure 5.3 shows the duty stations of the U.S. active-duty armed forces over the course of the second half of the century. Even during the Korean and Vietnam conflicts, about two-thirds of all active-duty forces were stationed inside the United States, engaged in logistics and supply, transportation, training, record-keeping, maintenance, and a host of other non-combat duties.

Outside of those conflict years, fully three-fourths of all active-duty soldiers have been stationed inside the United States. Another one-sixth of our armed forces occupied long-term bases and other facilities in Europe as part of our standing peacetime military presence in NATO and other alliances. Figure 5.2 above showed that the total intensity of military service for the Lucky Few rivals that of the Good Warriors, making them our two "military generations" of the century. However, while three-fourths of the Good Warrior time in uniform came during wartime, over two-thirds of the Lucky Few military service as a whole came during peacetime.

Elvis Presley, born in 1935, received his draft notice in 1957 just as he was preparing to film his movie *King Creole*. Although the draft board gave him a few months' extension to film the movie, in 1958 he reported for active duty in the Army and his income dropped from $400,000 to $78 per month. After six months of training with

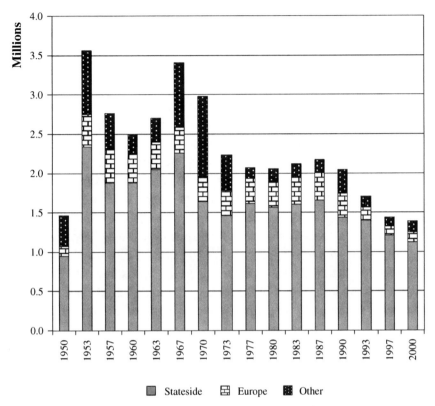

Fig. 5.3 Location of standing armed forces, 1950–2000
Source: Historical Statistics of the United States.

his tank unit at Fort Hood in Texas, Elvis completed the next year and a half of his peacetime military service as a jeep driver stationed in Germany, almost an ordinary soldier. His commanders got a lesson in the "almost" aspect, however, when they assigned him to guard duty one night and had to send platoons of men to rescue him from a sea of fans who surrounded his guard post. Elvis never pulled guard duty again. Johnny Cash, another Lucky Few recording star, already had completed his peacetime tour of duty at the U.S. Air Force base in Landsberg, Germany before Elvis received his draft notice – Cash had enlisted in the early 1950s. At about the same time that Elvis was heading for Germany in uniform, Lucky Few member Colin Powell graduated from the City College of New York with a bachelor's degree in geology. As an ROTC cadet, he received his commission as a second lieutenant in the U.S.

Army. The Army became his career for the remainder of the century, culminating in his appointment as the Chairman of the Joint Chiefs of Staff, the highest military position in the country, during which he coordinated Operation Desert Storm as noted in Chapter 1 above.

Over 36,000 U.S. soldiers died in the Korean conflict according to Defence Department figures. Most of the men who fought and died in Korea came from the Lucky Few because they dominated the battlefield ages, so we might estimate that roughly 30,000 Lucky Few men died during the Korean conflict. If so, this means that "their war" cost about 15 Lucky Few lives for every ten thousand of this generation's men. By the same sort of calculations, World War II cost about 180 lives for every ten thousand Good Warrior men, a fraction *twelve times higher* than for the Lucky Few in Korea. Even though they had their own war, as all generations seem to have, the Lucky Few made it past this harrowing feature of adulthood with the same relative good fortune that they have enjoyed in other aspects of their lives.

The Vietnam Conflict

United States participation in the conflict in Vietnam began while the area was still unravelling from the French colonial empire. In 1953 (several months before the armistice ending the Korean conflict was signed) the United States contributed 60 million dollars to assist French efforts aimed at putting down a guerrilla war being waged by Ho Chi Minh and other communist revolutionaries. While many Vietnamese saw the conflict as a struggle to end the colonial power of France, the conflict quickly took on overtones of a proxy war supplied and sponsored by the communist-led Russian and Chinese governments on one side and the western allies (including both France and the United States) on the other. The conflict escalated, but France proved hopelessly unable to suppress the revolution brewing in the country. The United States gradually stepped in and took the lead on the anti-communist side. At first this took the form of military advisors sent by President Kennedy in 1962 to guide the South Vietnamese forces, but as under French tutelage this approach quickly proved futile. By 1965 Kennedy had been assassinated, the still-debated Gulf of Tonkin incident had occurred, President Lyndon Johnson began aerial bombing of North Vietnam, and the first U.S. Marines landed as combat troops.

In that year the generational picture essentially had advanced one frame. In Vietnam the Baby Boomers occupied virtually the same position that the Lucky Few had occupied at the start of the Korean conflict. Baby Boomers filled all ages from 17 to 21 in 1967, while the last and youngest members of the Lucky Few who had chosen military careers found themselves in command as senior enlisted men and officers. Thus John Kerry (one of the youngest of the Lucky Few) commanded a swiftboat on the Mekong River, but his crew were mostly Baby Boomers. By 1973 when American forces finally gave up the hopeless task of trying to stop the unravelling of the old French empire (as the French had already done a decade before them) the youngest member of the Lucky Few was already 28 years old, well beyond the heart of the battlefield ages.

Nearly nine million men in all served in the military over the six or seven years of American involvement in the Vietnam conflict, again following the new rotation strategy that saw troops cycling in and out of the combat zone continuously. Nearly sixty thousand soldiers died in Vietnam, almost twice as many as died in the Korean conflict. During the years of heaviest fighting, from 1968 to 1972, Baby Boomers occupied nearly all the battlefield ages of 17–24 and so sustained most of these casualties – perhaps 50,000 of the deaths, with the other eight or nine thousand adding to the toll borne by the Lucky Few. Of course, there were a lot more Baby Boomers in the population, too, so the total impact of Vietnam on the Baby Boom generation of men actually resembled the impact of Korea on the Lucky Few – thirteen lives lost per ten thousand Baby Boom men, compared to fifteen lives lost per ten thousand Lucky Few men. Neither of these generations experienced anything like the casualties sustained by the Good Warrior generation in World War II.

The years of military service per 100 person-years lived between ages 17 and 54 shown above in Fig. 5.2 overstate the service record of the Baby Boom generation. This happens because the youngest Baby Boomers were still only 36 years old in 2000, when we stop counting years lived and years of service. The oldest Baby Boomers had just reached our cutoff age of 54, but the younger members of the generation still had many person-years left to live, inflating the denominator of our calculation. These additional person-years lived after 2000 come at older ages (in the forties and fifties) where very few men are still on active duty, so by the time the entire generation passes age 54, the intensity of service shown in the Figure will be considerably lower, rivalling the low levels observed among the Hard Timers and New Worlders. For the same reason, we do not even attempt to measure this intensity for Generation X.

Operation Desert Storm

To complete the picture of military service during the twentieth century we must take note of the final major conflict waged with American involvement, the 1991 Operation Desert Storm that drove Saddam Hussein's Iraqi forces out of Kuwait after they had invaded and occupied that oil-rich country in 1990. A quick look back at Fig. 5.1 reveals no major spike in military manpower at the start of the century's final decade. The United States managed to participate in the conflict without re-starting the draft or even producing any noticeable buildup in its armed forces at all. A slight rise in the surface of that graph in 1991 might be detected by the careful observer, but there is nothing to compare with earlier conflicts.

On this smaller scale, then, Operation Desert Storm involved Generation X at a point in their lives similar to that experienced by the Baby Boomers in Vietnam, the Lucky Few in Korea, the Good Warriors in the Second World War, the Hard Timers in the First World War, and the New Worlders at the time of the Spanish-American War. As in all these conflicts, a young generation concentrated in the battlefield ages did most of the actual fighting and suffered most of the casualties. Generation X occupied all ages from 19 to 36 in 1991 at the time of Desert Storm. As in all conflicts, older generations also were present, mostly as senior leaders. Generation X comprised 54 percent of the active-duty forces of the United States in 1991, alongside 44 percent of those forces who were Baby Boomers and a senior group of Lucky Few totalling only two percent of the military ranks (but including many of the commanding generals and admirals, including Colin Powell, Norman Schwartzkopf, Wesley Clark and others).

Casualties

Soldiers serving in the uniform of their country always risk making the ultimate sacrifice for their fellow citizens – they may lose their lives in combat. If this risk of death had remained unchanged for soldiers throughout the century, we could simply infer the relative risks of losses for each generation from the number of men serving in each generation, of course taking into account the amount of time they were exposed to such risks.

However, we already know that improvements in sanitation, medical research, better transportation and logistics, and even the increasing automation of warfare have drastically changed the risk of actually dying in combat experienced by soldiers of different generations. The sections above spell out generational contrasts in the share of adult lifetimes spent in military service. To assess the risk of death, we need to be more specific about who actually experienced this risk in a serious, tangible way. Consequently, we calculate the actual hazard of death in combat by comparing recorded deaths to the number of person-years lived as soldiers in uniform by each generation. We further restrict the definition by counting only person-years lived during wartime, and by counting only those men in the battlefield ages from 17 to 24 where the overwhelming bulk of all combat fatalities concentrate.

Figure 5.4 shows the remarkable improvements made in survival on the battlefield over the course of the twentieth century. By the end of the century, the American military was doing a far better job of protecting the lives of its soldiers than had been the case a hundred years earlier, reducing the risk of death per year of active duty in the battlefield ages during wartime to about *one-tenth* of the level experienced at the start of the century.

Selective Service

The Lucky Few were the *only* generation in American history to live with an active military draft as a permanent fixture of their lives for almost the entire time they were of military age, persisting through both peacetime and wartime. For the Hard Timers and Good Warriors before them, the draft came as a sudden surprise at the outbreak of

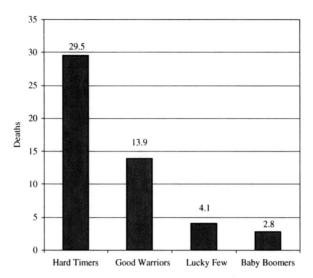

Fig. 5.4 Combat deaths per 1000 person-years of active duty in battlefield ages (17–24) during wartime
Source: Calculated from deaths reported in Military Manpower Statistics combined with active-duty information from Fig. 5.1 above.

each World War. After each war ended, massive demobilization was matched by relative inactivity of draft boards. For example, although the Selective Service registration system continued in effect after the Second World War, in 1947 not a single American was drafted.

Similarly, as the Vietnam war stumbled toward its awkward conclusion in the early 1970s, debate continued in American society about the logic underlying the peacetime draft. In 1973 the draft (which had helped to stimulate military service by the Lucky Few even in peacetime) was suspended. The United States converted to an all-volunteer military, following the recommendations (1970) of a special Presidential blue-ribbon commission formed to look into the issue. This fundamental shift in military manpower policy to an all-volunteer armed force had many long-term consequences, but for Baby Boomers the main result came quickly. The absence of any possibility of a draft no doubt partly explains why the level of military service for Baby Boomers fell back to levels seen for the earliest generations of the century.

Since Lucky Few men were subject to the military draft throughout early adulthood, participation in the armed forces tended to cut across social classes and other dimensions of difference in the population, just as had been true for the Good Warriors. In fact, for both of these mid-century "military generations" such service may have proven to be an asset in many ways after military duties were finished. For example, every President of the United States elected from the Good Warrior generation (John Kennedy, Richard Nixon, Gerald Ford, Ronald Reagan, Jimmy Carter and George H.W. Bush) as well as the Hard Timer President in their midst (Lyndon Johnson) put forward a record of military service as a fundamental strength or qualification to hold our nation's highest elective office. For Good Warriors and the Lucky Few, the G.I. Bills passed by Congress provided support and opportunities for veterans to move ahead in higher education, opportunities not available to their contemporaries without military service records.

Many economists and demographers who have studied the job histories of veterans and non-veterans (Martindale & Poston 1979) find a veteran "premium" in later lifetime earnings. Some writers (DeTray 1982) suggest that this earnings advantage results from the selectivity of military service – to serve in the military, one must pass certain physical and psychological tests that reject some people, so we might expect those selected as soldiers to have done better in life even if they had never been in the military. However, the debate continues (Angrist & Krueger 1994) about whether the higher earnings of veterans result from such selectivity into the armed forces, from special skills and experience gained during military service, or also possibly from advantages extended to veterans after they leave military service.

To disentangle these possible effects, researchers have compared the formal schooling achieved by veterans and non-veterans in each generation. For comparability we look at each generation at roughly the same ages considered in Chapter 3 above when discussing education, this time adding information about veteran status. We observe the Hard Timers at ages 32–50 in the 1940 Census, the Good Warriors at ages 32–51 in the 1960 Census, The Lucky Few at ages 35–51 in the 1980 Census, and the Baby Boomers at ages 31–49 in the 1995 Current Population Survey conducted by the Census Bureau.

Figure 5.5 shows the selective advantage of military service very clearly in the case of high school dropouts. In every generation of adult men, veterans include a much smaller proportion of high school

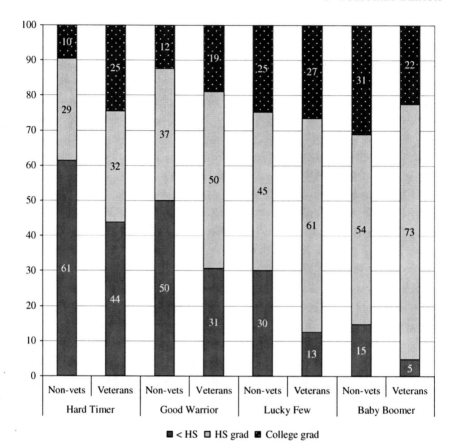

Fig. 5.5 Men's education by veteran status
Source: Hard Timers from 1940 Census PUMS file (ages 32 – 50), Good
Warriors from 1960 PUMS file (ages 32 – 51), Lucky Few from 1980 PUMS
file (ages 35 – 51), Baby Boomers from 1995 CPS file (ages 31 – 49).

dropouts than observed in the rest of the male population. Figure 5.5
shows an approximate one-generation lag in high school completion
for non-veterans compared to veterans; to put this in perspective,
chapter 8 documents a similar one-generation education lag between
blacks and whites in twentieth-century America. Even when a high
school diploma was not formally required for military service, knowledge learned in high school was important for being able to pass the
armed forces entrance examination. People with impoverished, uned-
ucated backgrounds also had a higher share of physical problems that
might disqualify them from military service.

   The share of men graduating from college among veterans versus
non-veterans tells a very different story. Here we encounter the Lucky
Few as the last members of an old pattern that has disappeared. Lucky
Few veterans (like veterans from the Good Warrior and Hard Timer
generations before them) not only were more likely to finish high
school; they also were more likely to graduate from college than were
men who had not served in the military. In part this might reflect the
same selection of people with more physical and mental strengths into
the armed forces. In part it also may reflect the special efforts made to
assist veterans to return to successful civilian lives after serving their
country, through programs like the GI Bill support of higher education
(Nam, 1964).
   Among the Baby Boomer men this college graduation advantage
for veterans disappeared. In spite of continued veterans' programs
in education, job training and other assistance (as well as subsi-
dized health care for veterans), Baby Boomer men who served in
the armed forces were sharply less likely to finish college by the
time they reached middle age than were the civilians in their generation who never served in the military. This turnaround undoubtedly reflects the end of the draft and the introduction of an all-
volunteer military in the early 1970s, and the resulting very low
rates of military experience among Baby Boomers. Not only has
this generation experienced less military service than any generation since the Hard Timers or New Worlders at the beginning of
the century, but for Baby Boomers, military service has been "selective" in a very different sense. Boomers with higher education,
good career prospects, and generally advantageous positions in life
are most likely to have skipped military service. Poorer, less-educated
Americans are more likely to have joined the new all-volunteer military. This negative economic selection into the military did not exist among the Good Warriors or the Lucky Few, at least not to anything like the same extent. No amount of programmatic assistance
for veterans has been able to reverse such negative selection effects. Boomer men with military experience have been much less
likely than non-military men to finish college. Further, the same economic studies that find a veterans' bonus in lifetime earnings for all
generations of soldiers prior to the Baby boom also find that this
earnings bonus has disappeared for the Baby Boom and for Generation X (so far as we can tell at this early stage of their lives),

and that in fact there is now a lifetime earnings *penalty* attached
to military service (Martindale & Poston 1979, Angrist & Krueger
1994).

Veterans

As a result of these very different generational experiences with
active-duty military service, each generation of the twentieth century
has reached maturity with its own distinctive life history. Figure 5.6
clarifies the pattern across generations, showing the passage of the
Good Warrior generation through the century with about two-thirds
of all men declaring themselves to be military veterans, even reaching
a peak of three-fourths of all men for the central birth cohorts that
were most involved in the Good War.

By comparison to the Good Warriors, military service by all other
generations was less salient in their lives. Only about one-fourth of the
Hard Timers identified themselves in later censuses as veterans from

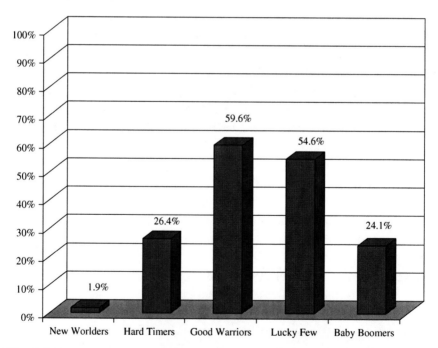

Fig. 5.6 Percent veterans among men by generation (census self-reports)
Source: Original calculations from Census Public Use Microdata Samples.

the First World War. This same one-fourth share appears again for Baby Boomer men who identify themselves as veterans of Vietnam and other military service of their era. Figures for the New Worlders at the dawn of the century and Generation X at its close continue this pattern, showing even less military involvement than for the Hard Timers or Baby Boomers.

The Lucky Few occupy an intermediate position between the war-centered Good Warrior generation and the other less-militarized generations of the century. Over half of Lucky Few men identify themselves as military veterans. As noted above, some of the oldest Lucky Few veterans fought in Korea at the very beginning of their generation's passage through ages of military service, while some of the youngest Lucky Few veterans saw action in Vietnam, often as officers and senior enlisted personnel leading the Baby Boom into that conflict.

The great majority of Lucky Few veterans, however, served like Elvis in the massive new standing peacetime armed forces of the United States, during the 14 years between 1953 and 1967 when the country was not engaged in any large-scale military conflicts anywhere in the world. If we count each Lucky Few soldier who served in each year that any of them were in the ages between 17 and 54, about two-thirds (64 percent) of these "person-years" of military duty came during peacetime years. Fifteen percent of Lucky Few service person-years took place during the Korean conflict, mostly in the battlefield ages, and the remaining 21 percent of Lucky Few service person-years took place during Vietnam, mostly at ages well above the battlefield ages.

Most Lucky Few soldiers (even during their wartime years) served garrison duty in the far-flung posts of the U.S. military presence around the world, including the massive peacetime military establishment within the United States itself. Although much less involved in actual warfare, the considerable peacetime service of Lucky Few soldiers in the standing armed forces meant that in the end, the total level of Lucky Few participation in the military did not fall very far short of the Good Warriors, involving twice as big a share of the Lucky Few generation than was true for the Baby Boomers or Generation X who followed them and also twice as high as for the Hard Timers who fought in World War I.

This means that a large share of Lucky Few men qualify for veterans' benefits in medical care, military pensions, and other rewards for military service. At the same time, the casualties experienced by these peacetime patriots fell far short of the losses among the Good Warriors – the risk of wartime deaths for Lucky Few men was only a small fraction of the risk experienced by the Good Warriors. The level of casualties for the Lucky Few was about the same as the level for the Baby Boomers, but the Lucky Few are twice as likely as Baby Boomers to be veterans and to be eligible for the benefits accorded to those who have served their country in uniform.

Chapter 6
High Road to Money and Power

Contents

As detailed in the preceding chapter, over half of the Lucky Few men spent part of their early adult lives in military service. Most Lucky Few soldiers served peacetime tours of duty as Elvis did, or spent their time stateside during periods of active warfare, as in the case of Clint Eastwood in California. War did not give this generation its signature theme as had been the case for the Great Warriors before them. Instead, the lifelong motif for the Lucky Few generation really began to emerge as they pursued their careers in civilian life, already examined briefly in Chapter 4. We begin this chapter with a look at the changes in the social and economic landscape that greeted them as they embarked on their unparalleled economic successes in adulthood.

The Postwar Economic Boom

The Lucky Few finished school and embarked on their careers just in time for the largest and longest economic boom in American history. The U.S. economy changed dramatically in the second half of the twentieth century, compared to how things had progressed in earlier decades. Figure 6.1 shows the trend in the per-capita Gross Domestic

E. Carlson, *The Lucky Few*,
© Springer Science+Business Media B.V. 2008

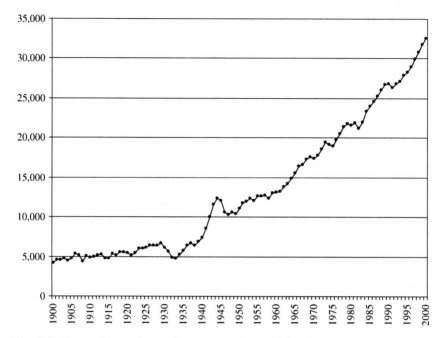

Fig. 6.1 Gross domestic product per capita (1996 dollars)
Source: Historical Statistics of the United States, Millenial Edition Online,
Series CA9-19.

Product (GDP), an index economists use to measure the volume of
transactions in American society in relation to the population. GDP
per capita provides a good measure of the average economic value created by each person in the United States year-by-year. Since the real
purchasing power of wages and prices changed dramatically over the
decades, this series (like most federal statistics) has been adjusted by
government economists using a "price deflator" that converts dollars
in different years to what they would have purchased in one chosen
index year (1996 for Fig. 6.1).

    The line on this graph appears rather flat until the end of World
War II, just when the Lucky Few generation began to finish school,
get married, and start looking for jobs as discussed in earlier chapters.
At that point the Gross Domestic Product per person began to expand
steadily. The steep upward slope of this line for the entire second half
of the twentieth century presents a clear picture of economic expansion and rising prosperity throughout the working lives of the Lucky

Few generation. Despite some "wobbles" in the series, such as the slight dip at the time of the oil crisis in the mid-1970s, rising productivity of the American economy laid the foundation for unparalleled career prospects enjoyed by the Lucky Few. They never again experienced anything like the hard childhood years some of them witnessed during the 1930s. The depression years that so affected the working lives and mentalities of adult Hard Timers and the oldest Good Warriors remained only as childhood memories for the oldest of the Lucky Few.

Occupational Transformation of the Labor Force

Each generation living through the twentieth century encountered a different social landscape as they sought their places in the nation's huge, complex system of jobs and businesses. Growing accumulation of wealth, scientific and technological progress, the expansion of corporations, rising levels of education in the population, the shift of people from the countryside into metropolitan areas, and a host of other changes guaranteed that no two generations experienced the transition to adulthood alike over the course of the century.

Chapter 3 showed that the New Worlders included many people (including many foreign-born immigrants) who lived in rural America. Even though they sometimes moved off the farms to take urban jobs, many New Worlders remained in rural areas throughout their lives. Figure 6.2 shows this rural farm aspect of life for New Worlders captured by the 1920 Census at ages 31–49 (that is, in mid-life when most people have settled into the occupations they will pursue as adults). The large dark-shaded segment at the base of the column representing their occupations shows that more than one-fifth of all New Worlder men worked as farmers. By comparison, later generations clearly abandoned farming almost completely. Only a fraction of one percent of Baby Boomer men enumerated by the 2000 Census at ages 36–54 were still farming. Note, however, that "farmers" do not include farm workers, hired hands, or day-laborers. These people who work the land without owning it or having permanent residences there appear instead in the "laborers" category in the figure.

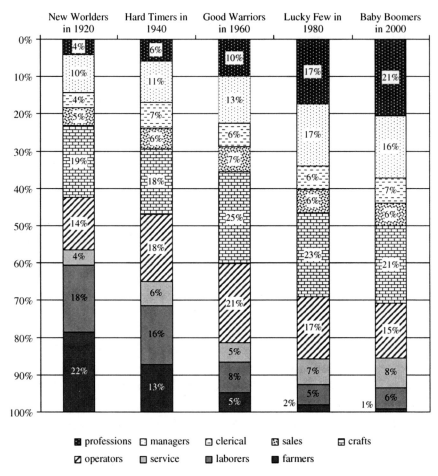

Fig. 6.2 Occupations of men in mid-life
Source: Original calculations from Census Public Use Microdata Samples.

After the New Worlders, the segments representing farmers shown
in Fig. 6.2 shrink dramatically for Hard Timer and for Good Warrior
men. This farm exodus took place without much compensating expansion of the top three or four categories – the so-called "white-collar"
occupations of clerical and sales workers and managers, and professional and technical workers whose jobs involve advanced education
and training. These observations fit in with the point made about education of the generations in Chapter 3, since these early generations
lacked the high school and/or college degrees needed for many white-
collar jobs.

If farming did not give way to professional or management jobs, where did Hard Timer and Good Warrior men work instead? Figure 6.2 clearly shows that as men moved to the new industrial cities of America, they took jobs as operators of factory machinery, industrial equipment, motor vehicles, and other blue-collar jobs in place of farming. Even more dramatically, the Good Warrior men moved in massive numbers into craft occupations, becoming carpenters, repairmen, electricians, masons, machinists, plumbers, painters, upholsterers, cabinet-makers, opticians, and a host of other skilled workers. A larger share of Good Warrior men worked as craftsmen than for any other twentieth-century generation.

For the New Worlders, Hard Timers and Good Warriors alike, less than one-fourth of all men found careers as managers, officials or in the professions. If Good Warrior men led a shift from farms to urban blue-collar jobs, the next shift from blue-collar to white-collar jobs and professions occurred for Lucky Few men. The big jump for these occupations in Fig. 6.2 comes between the Good Warriors and the Lucky Few. This makes sense in terms of the impressive leap forward in formal schooling already reported for Lucky Few men. Over one-third of all Lucky Few men became professionals or managers, rising quickly up through the new corporate organizations in which they found jobs right out of school, and going on in unprecedented numbers to successful careers in these fields. Baby Boomer men later essentially reproduced the occupational mix of the Lucky Few with a few minor shifts.

At first glance, the equivalent Fig. 6.3 showing occupations for generations of women seems paradoxical – the share of professionals among women always has been much higher in each generation than the share for men. This reflects the clumsy measurement ability of only a few broad occupational headings like these. In actuality, women in professions always have had a very different mix of specific jobs than male professionals. For women the leading professions through most of the twentieth century included nursing and teaching in elementary and high schools, while for men the leading professions included law, medicine, college and university teaching, and other higher-status, higher-paid jobs. Still, it remains true that the female labor force (small though it was at first) always has had a more "white-collar" character than the work force of men in the United States.

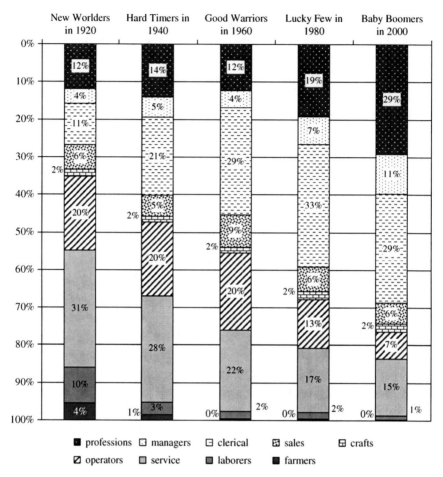

Fig. 6.3 Occupations of women in mid-life
Source: Original calculations from Census Public Use Microdata Samples.

Two other features of jobs for women also stand out from Fig. 6.3, showing dramatic differences across the generations. At the start of the century, among the small minority of New Worlder and Hard Timer women with paid jobs, most worked in service occupations— that is, jobs as maids, housecleaners, nannies, paid servants in homes, hired girls on farms, or as menial employees in hotels, office buildings or other settings. Women living and working beside their husbands on farms were not counted as "farmers," though, so the female labor force from those early days of the century was systematically undercounted. For New Worlder women, the second-most-likely sort of paying job would have been operating some sort of machine, often a sewing machine in a garment sweatshop or similar setting.

However, employment of women in industry as machine operators peaked among the still-small female labor force of the Good Warrior generation, just as it did for men. In the case of women, these factory jobs actually peaked during the Second World War when women took the place of men serving in the military. "Rosie the Riveter" symbolized the millions of women who went to work during wartime in America's industrial labor force. At the conclusion of the war much of this female industrial labor force was encouraged to return to their homes and "make room" for the returning men – one more aspect of the post-war scene that contributed to the Baby Boom and the era of motherhood mania already discussed in Chapter 3. Even in their peak working ages around age 50, we know from Chapter 4 that no more than about half of all Good Warrior women had paying jobs.

The share of women working in service jobs, the biggest single category for New Worlder women, shrank significantly for each succeeding generation. Instead, a new concentration of jobs in clerical occupations appeared for women in the later generations, as shown by the dramatic expansion of this category in Fig. 6.3. Some writers even call these clerical occupations the "pink-collar ghetto" because they absorbed so much of the rapidly-expanding female labor force.

Clerical work became the hallmark particularly of Lucky Few women. A full one-third of all Lucky Few women with paying jobs at ages 35–51 in 1980 (the peak working ages for their generation) reported clerical occupations. No other generation of women experienced such an intense concentration of jobs in this one occupational group. Perhaps it is fitting, then, that one of the most popular movie treatments of this working environment, *Nine to Five*, starred Lucky Few actresses Jane Fonda and Lily Tomlin (along with Baby Boomer Dolly Parton, whose birth in 1946 just missed placing her in the Lucky Few) as workers in the pink-collar ghetto. The film also featured Lucky Few actor Dabney Coleman as their clueless and chauvinistic male boss.

Though they usually took paying jobs only after their children were well along in school, Lucky Few women eventually did start a significant shift away from both blue-collar and service jobs. The apex of the "pink-collar ghetto" accounted for part of this shift, but Fig. 6.3 also shows important gains in both managerial and professional jobs for

Lucky Few women. This trend continued to accelerate when the Baby Boomer women with their substantial educational gains came on the scene. The "pink-collar ghetto" itself began to shrink as a result of computerization, office automation and other technological changes, so that the occupational distribution of Baby Boomer women actually resembles that of Baby Boomer men (except women still tend to have the secretarial jobs and men still tend to be the craftsmen and equipment operators).

By the end of the century, women had achieved rough parity with men in admissions to both law schools and medical schools, although enrollments in business schools still counted three or four men for every woman student. In terms of labor force participation, Lucky Few women achieved some of the biggest occupational changes of the century, just as we saw for Lucky Few men. While Lucky Few men shifted into management and the professions, Lucky Few women shifted out of service and blue-collar work into the pink-collar ghetto of clerical jobs. These patterns match what we might expect from their educational experiences.

Generational Participation in the Union Boom

Another dramatic change affecting the world of work during the twentieth century appears in Fig. 6.4, showing a remarkable "Union Boom" in the middle of the century that resulted in part from the occupational shifts described above. The Union Boom started shortly before the Baby Boom, but lasted twice as long – almost forty years rather than only twenty. The share of the employed population belonging to labor unions rose dramatically in the aftermath of the Great Depression, gaining tremendous ground during the Second World War as manufacturing industries expanded quickly under the stimulus of wartime production. The peak in union membership came shortly after mid-century, but then membership rates began to drop again as industrial employment itself declined. By the end of the century, American workers were just about back where they had started in 1900, with less than ten percent of the total employed population reporting union membership.

How did this Union Boom appear in the lives of our successive generations? Even a moment's reflection should give us a very good

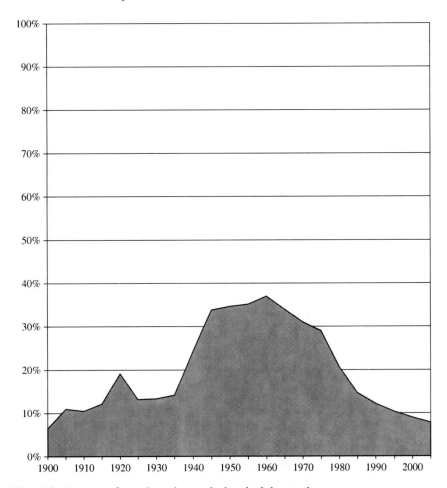

Fig. 6.4 Percent of employed population in labor unions
Source: Historical Statistics of the United States.

guess on this point. Figure 6.2 above just illustrated the fact that the
Good Warrior men made the biggest leap from farming to blue-collar
and crafts occupations – the kinds of jobs most likely to be involved
with labor union membership. On the other hand, the Lucky Few
men made the biggest jump of the century from blue-collar jobs to
white-collar occupations, management and the professions – walks
of life where union membership never took root to the extent it did
in blue-collar jobs. Therefore we would expect the Good Warriors to
be the champions of labor unions, and the Lucky Few to leave this
form of collective organization behind. This is precisely what we see

in Fig. 6.5, constructed from responses to a series of national surveys over the course of the century. In this Figure, the Union Boom clearly appears, distributed among our generations. Most generations appear twice in the figure, captured once at ages between roughly 25 and 45 when they are young workers, and again a couple of decades later (in the next survey) when they have reached mature working ages between roughly 45 and 65, and are beginning to look toward retirement. Only the New Worlders (already "mature workers" in the 1937 survey) and the Baby Boomers (just arrived as "young workers" in the data centered on 1989) are limited to a single measurement.

Figure 6.5 shows low union membership for the mature New Worlders early in the century, and low union membership again for the young Baby Boomers as they approached the end of the century.

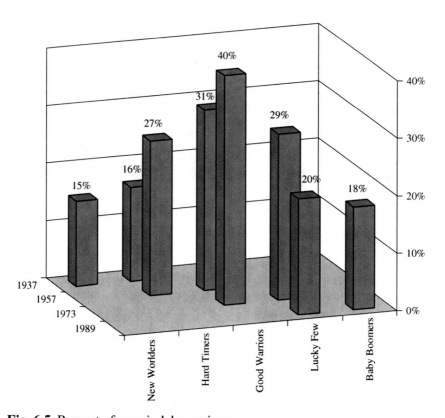

Fig. 6.5 Percent of men in labor unions
Source: Original calculations from Gallup Polls and General Social Surveys.

In between, the Union Boom appears among the Hard Timers, Good Warriors, and Lucky Few.

The Hard Timers ("young workers" in 1937 and "mature workers" in 1957) show us the upswing in industrial manufacturing and union jobs that resulted from World War II production and the post-war industrial boom. The Good Warriors ("young workers" in 1957 and "mature workers" in 1973) show us the peak of the Union Boom, as nearly four of every ten Good Warrior men reported belonging to a labor union by the later date. This remarkable result shows us yet another side of the Good Warriors, already united by the overwhelming extent of their wartime military service and by being (along with the Lucky Few) one of the two most native-born of all American generations. Since this generation produced more skilled craftsmen and industrial workers than any other generation in American history, it makes perfect sense that they also were by far the most unionized workers the country has ever seen.

The Lucky Few, already past the peak of blue-collar industrial employment in the country and rising into management and professional jobs on the basis of their higher education, never reached a level of union membership anywhere near that of the Good Warriors. Even as "young workers" in 1973, the Lucky Few men were only as unionized as the mature Hard Timers had been twenty years earlier–only a little over a fourth of them reported union membership. By the time they reached mature working ages, union membership among the Lucky Few actually fell by nearly a third, making them the first generation of the century to move away from unions as they grew older, rather than gaining more union membership with increasing age and job seniority. Mature Lucky Few workers were only about as likely to belong to unions as the young Baby Boomers.

Growth of Corporations

Not all transactions measured in the expanding Gross Domestic Product (shown above in Fig. 6.1) actually represent income earned directly by individual men and women. Ever since 1886, when the Supreme Court ruled in *Wabash, St. Louis and Pacific Railroad Company versus Illinois* that corporations are "persons" with rights guaranteed by the constitution, a new sort of population has been growing up alongside the human population of the United States. We are not talking about cats and dogs, but about corporations. If we could put on special legal spectacles that allowed us to see not only the flesh-and-blood people around us but also the "juridical persons" that are corporations, we would suddenly perceive ghostly forms standing or moving among us. Some of these wraith-like figures would be about the same size as real people – these could be, for example, the "shadow individuals" created when a doctor or a lawyer or an artist incorporates himself or herself for the purpose of doing business. Others would stand much larger. These larger-than-life juridical persons might include Exxon, General Motors, the Bank of America, Archer Daniels Midland or the Boeing Corporation.

These gigantic specters, even the very largest of them, move and act as great marionettes whose strings invariably can be traced to the hands of human members of the crowd. Sam Walton, a Good Warrior honor student and star athlete in high school, served with most of the rest of his generation in World War II. In the end, though, he is best-known as the founder of his huge, far-flung Walmart Corporation – a juridical person who has made Walton's family one of the richest in the world. Rupert Murdoch, the Australian tycoon who became an American citizen (and so might qualify as an "adopted" member of the Lucky Few, since he was born in 1931) still pulls the strings to operate his New York-based News Corporation empire that spans the globe with newspapers, television stations, and other media outlets.

Incorporated juridical persons (corporations) surely represent the greatest single legal innovation of the last two millennia (Micklethwait & Wooldridge 2005). No flesh-and-blood citizen in contemporary America (or most other countries) can live without continual and important interactions with them. Many of the economic transactions that contribute to the Gross Domestic Product involve people on one side and corporations on the other. When you pay your electric bill or make a car payment, for example, or when you buy groceries or purchase a movie ticket, you almost always are giving your money to a corporation. Many such transactions occur directly between corporations themselves, as when corporations guided by Lucky Few raider/entrepreneurs like Carl Icahn, Henry Kravis, Joseph Perella or Saul Steinberg purchase other corporations in leveraged buyouts and hostile takeovers. Real people always sign the papers, but in such cases they are acting only as agents and employees of these "juridical persons."

As shown in Fig. 6.6, the second half of the twentieth century witnessed an explosion of the corporate population. Between 1950 and the end of the century, during the careers of the Lucky Few, the population of corporations in America grew at an average annual rate of 5.2 percent, many times faster than the population of actual people. This "compound-interest" expansion of corporations continues to follow an exponential track that doubles their number every twelve to fifteen years. At that rate, there would be one corporation for every person in the United States shortly after the middle of the 21st century. Nothing like this has ever been seen in economic history before.

The mushrooming growth of new corporate business, pioneered in many cases by Lucky Few entrepreneurs, provided the job growth needed to absorb America's expanding population. As the labor force

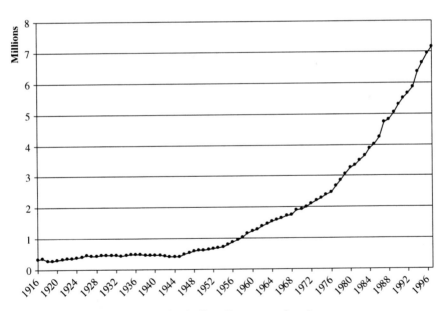

Fig. 6.6 U.S. corporations (including S-corporations)
Source: U.S. Internal Revenue Service (and its predecessor, U.S. Bureau of Internal Revenue), *Statistics of Income (SOI)*, various issues; *SOI Bulletin*, various issues.

expanded rapidly in the second half of the century, these new companies hired the lion's share of the new workers.

At mid-century, for example, less than 50 million Americans held paying jobs. About 60 percent of them (about 30 million) worked as employees of established businesses, rather than working for themselves as proprietors or independent contractors or professionals. These figures from the Economic Censuses of the United States – formerly known as the Census of Business – include all firms with employees, not only incorporated businesses. Firms with employees did show an increasing tendency to incorporate as the century passed, so more of the employees at mid-century worked directly for real flesh-and-blood individual employers, rather than for corporations.

By the end of the century the number of working Americans had more than doubled to over 120 million people, of whom fully three-fourths (about 90 million) worked as employees in businesses rather than on their own. This means that the number of employees tripled over five decades, from 30 to 90 million, while the number of self-employed workers rose only from about 20 to about 30 million. The bulk of all jobs added in the American economy during these decades of phenomenal growth were created for employees in large and growing companies, and a rising share of those companies were incorporated as juridical "persons" in their own right.

While many of the Lucky Few merely took corporate jobs, some of the leading entrepreneurs in this well-placed generation were more fortunate – they took over or actually created the corporations themselves. After a privileged childhood with his wealthy family in Manhattan and attendance at a sequence of private schools and colleges, Michael Eisner (born 1942) immediately parlayed his 1964 BA in English from Denison University into jobs in New York at all three of the major broadcast networks – first NBC, then CBS, and finally ABC. Within seven years Eisner had risen to the post of Vice President for Daytime Programming at ABC, and then within a few years more to Senior Vice President for Program Planning and Development. Many of the programs he introduced, such as *Happy Days* and *Welcome Back Kotter*, probably will live forever in syndication.

At the peak of his ABC career, however, Eisner jumped to Paramount Pictures to join an old friend and colleague there, and as chief operating officer of Paramount he brought the world the *Star Trek* television series and films, *Saturday Night Fever*, the *Raiders of the Lost Ark* films, the *Beverly Hills Cop* films, and countless others. Eisner might have remained at Paramount, but when he was passed over for the studio's top job in 1984, at the age of 42 he jumped again to the Walt Disney Company (which until then had been owned and operated largely by the Disney family). This move was not quite as successful, partly because he feuded with a rival executive hired at the same time and partly because the Disney family proved reluctant to give up day-to-day control of the company. Still, Eisner recognized the same formula for success that worked for many other Lucky Few executives who piloted growing corporations in late 20th-century America – produce something that will appeal to the enormous Baby Boom generation coming along behind the Lucky Few, and your products will sell like hotcakes. Throughout his career Eisner produced television programs and motion pictures particularly aimed at Boomers, but the principle has worked for many kinds of goods and services.

Ted Turner (Auletta 2005) presents a slightly different version of the Lucky Few media entrepreneur, though in many respects similar to Michael Eisner. Born Robert Edward Turner in Cincinnati in 1938, young Ted also attended exclusive private schools and colleges, including Brown University. He began his media career involuntarily when his father's 1963 suicide left him in charge of the family's Atlanta business (the Turner Billboard Company) shortly before his 25th birthday. Within a decade he used the resources of this million-dollar company to buy a UHF television station in Atlanta, later adding his well-known Cable News Network (CNN) and then Turner Network Television (TNT) and Turner Classic Movies (TCM) television channels. Like another Lucky Few entrepreneur (Domino's Pizza founder Thomas Monaghan, who bought the Detroit Tigers), Turner added professional sports teams to his investment portfolio, calling his Atlanta Braves "America's team." Unlike the extremely conservative Monaghan, though, Turner has pursued a distinctly liberal agenda in his philanthropic and political endeavors, demonstrating that although the Lucky Few have been a generally conservative generation (see the next chapter), each generation includes the entire diverse political spectrum even among its elites.

The very comfortable origins of both Eisner and Turner might give the impression that most great entrepreneurs among the Lucky Few started out with silver spoons in their mouths, but such an impression is just as wrong as the idea that all Lucky Few are conservatives.

Many of the Lucky Few's most successful business leaders came from humble beginnings, including Thomas Monaghan mentioned above. As another example, John Francis Welch, Jr. (better known as Jack) was born in 1935 to a Catholic railroad conductor and his wife in the suburbs of Boston (Welch & Byrne 2001). He trained initially as a chemical engineer at the University of Massachusetts at Amherst and then at the University of Illinois. With his PhD in hand in 1960, he went directly to work for General Electric Corporation, but he was not destined to remain a chemical engineer.

Senior company officials went out of their way to retain and promote him, and within 12 years he had been elected as a vice-president of the company. Five years later he had become the Senior Vice President, and in 1981 became the youngest CEO ever to control the General Electric Corporation. As head of General Electric, Welch quickly earned a ferocious reputation. He reorganized and reduced staff ruthlessly and continuously, shutting down inefficient plants and sections of the business, reducing inventories, and constantly demanding more performance from all levels of employees and management through a motivational mixture of rewards and fear.

Within two decades, nearly a third of the employees of General Electric disappeared and the profits of the corporation multiplied more than five-fold over the 1980 level. By his retirement in 2004, the market value of GE had blossomed from $14 billion to $410 billion, making it the largest and most valuable corporation on the planet at that time. He made some investments, of course, such as GE's purchase of the National Broadcasting Corporation in 1986, but first and foremost he excelled as a corporate manager. In fact, Forbes Magazine selected "Neutron Jack" Welch as the Manager of the Century.

Generational Investments in Corporations

A significant fraction of the income earned by "persons" in American society actually passes into the hands of these juridical persons in the form of corporate profits left over after paying flesh-and-blood employees and other expenses. The per capita denominator used to compare the Gross Domestic Product to the population does not include these juridical persons, but their incomes count in the numerator. According to the Bureau of Economic Analysis, over the second half of the twentieth century a steady 20 percent of all income earned in the United States took the form of profits earned by corporations. By comparison, 50 percent of all income earned in the country across these decades represents wages and salaries of individual workers in the private sector. Wages and salaries of local, state and federal government workers add up to another steady 10 percent of all incomes. Independent small business owners and landlords split the remaining 20 percent of all income as profits from unincorporated businesses and as rents respectively. Not only is it important, then, to look at income actually earned directly by people in each generation, but ideally we also would like to see each generation's participation in the ownership and control of the incorporated legal persons who receive one-fifth of all the income in the country and control far more than one-fifth of all the accumulated wealth.

All corporate stock ultimately is owned by flesh-and-blood individuals, and research consistently has shown that such investments have increased in value over the long term faster than any other form of invested wealth. To what extent have our different twentieth-century generations participated as owners of the expanding population of corporations? To what extent did Good Warriors, the Lucky Few, Baby Boomers and all the rest manage to share in the 20 percent of the GDP accruing to these juridical persons? As it turns out, the Lucky Few again appear lucky in this respect – they enjoyed the biggest collective jump in stock ownership of any generation during the century.

We can get a rough idea about investments of generations by looking at the series of Surveys of Consumer Finances (SCF) conducted every three years by the Federal Reserve Board. The earliest available SCF data, from 1962, show us the Good Warriors in the midst of their mature working years (at ages 34–53). The SCF data from 1983 similarly captured the Lucky Few at ages 37–53, and the 2001 Survey found Baby Boomers age ages 37–55. These three "snapshots" of successive generations, each framed squarely in the midst of their careers, reveal the extent to which each of them had been able to translate economic achievements into investments for the future (including investments for their own comforts in old age, as discussed below in Chapter 9).

People can own corporate stock directly as individuals (as was the case for almost 90 percent of all stock in 1950, at the middle of the century), or they can own the shares indirectly, when they invest their money in a corporation (especially a mutual fund or other investment business) that indirectly purchases stock in other corporations (Poterba et al. 1995. In 1962, the few Good Warriors who owned shares of stock in corporations mostly had purchased these stocks directly as individuals. Investments in mutual funds, holding collections of stocks indirectly for their investors, were still uncommon at that time. Fewer than one-fourth of all households headed by Good Warriors in 1962 reported owning any stock in either of these ways. The older Hard Timers, already making the transition to retirement at about this time, reported a similar level of investment involving between one-fifth and one-fourth of all their households.

By 1983, as the Lucky Few reached mid-career ages, the share of Lucky Few households with stock investments had roughly doubled compared to the 1962 levels attained by Good Warrior households at similar ages. Individual direct investment in stocks increased slightly across these decades or generations, but the real change involved new opportunities, new ways of investing that came about just when the Lucky Few were ready to take advantage of them. As Poterba et al. (1995) and a host of others have shown, this expansion of investment had much to do with the introduction in the 1970s of another new financial idea, the Individual Retirement Account (including Keogh Plans and other investment vehicles). These IRA accounts frequently were invested indirectly through mutual funds, rather than through direct purchases of individual stocks. Due to high employment rates (discussed in Chapter 4 above) and higher incomes from their white-collar, managerial and professional occupations discussed earlier in this chapter, many of the Lucky Few were in excellent positions to pioneer these new wealth-building investment options. Figure 6.7 illustrates the share of households in these generations with direct individual investments in corporate stock, and the larger shares of stockholders that appear when we also count participation in mutual funds and IRAs.

Warren Buffett, one of these Lucky Few investment pioneers, eventually became one of the world's richest men. Born in 1930, by age eleven he already had started working informally in his stock broker/congressman father's brokerage firm in Omaha, Nebraska, where he bought his first share of stock (in Cities Services). Even before entering the prestigious Wharton Business School at the University of Pennsylvania, Buffet owned a 40-acre farm purchased with his

Fig. 6.7 Corporate
stock ownership
(households by
generation of
householder)
Source: Original
calculations from
1962, 1983 and 2001
Surveys of Consumer
Finances, Federal
Reserve Board.

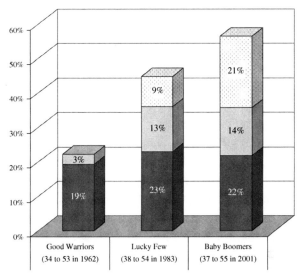

paper-route earnings, which he rented out to farmers (Kilpatrick 2001).
He was not drafted during the Korean conflict, and by 1951 had earned
a Masters degree in business at Columbia University. He returned
to his home in Omaha to continue working for his father – and to
marry Susan Thompson in 1952. After a short stint in the New York
investment firm of his famous Columbia business professor, Benjamin
Graham, Buffett again returned home to Omaha and founded several
partnerships. For a decade he continued to invest and build wealth,
until in 1962 he discovered a quiet, undervalued little textile company
called Berkshire Hathaway.

Over the next three years, Buffett and his associates aggressively
bought up the company's stock, taking over in 1965. A few years later
he liquidated all his partnership assets and concentrated on Berkshire
Hathaway. Within a decade his shares were worth a hundred times
what he had paid for them, and he had transformed the corporation
from a sleepy textile firm to a holding company investing in other
firms such as the New York Times Corporation, Coca Cola, and many
other corporations based on his famous investment guidelines.

Charles Schwab, born into the home of a Sacramento lawyer in
1937 just after the deepest crisis years of the Great Depression, furnishes another version of the successful preoccupation of the Lucky
Few with the new corporate America. Despite his dyslexia, his ability and determination propelled Schwab through Stanford University

where he studied economics and emerged in 1961 with MBA in hand
at precisely the right historical moment. After several years working
as a mutual funds manager, he established his own investment brokerage in San Francisco in 1971 at the ripe old age of 34. Unlike
Buffet, he concentrated on appealing to growing numbers of small
investors by offering low transaction costs and fees. His discount
brokerage became one of the best-known and most successful in the
United States.

In 2001, Baby Boomers (viewed at roughly the same ages as the
earlier generations in earlier years) were almost exactly as likely as
the Lucky Few to have invested in these same forms of corporate
ownership – direct individual stock purchases, mutual funds, and IRA
accounts. However, by the end of the century yet another kind of
investment vehicle – the defined-contribution retirement plan – had
appeared. Figure 6.7 above also shows participation by the Lucky
Few and the Baby Boomers in this new way of investing: payroll
deductions by employers purchase conventional mutual fund shares
in the employee's name, often with matching contributions from the
employers in place of a conventional pension contract.

If we add in this new kind of investments, a greater share of Baby
Boomers reported owning stock in one of these many ways than even
the Lucky Few had managed. As the next section of this chapter makes
clear, however, such defined-contribution pension programs which involve actual stock purchases in many cases have replaced an earlier
type of defined-benefit pension plan that did not involve actual stock
purchases by employees themselves – plans more available to earlier
generations. If we consider only directly-held stocks, mutual funds
and IRAs without the new defined-benefit retirement programs, the
Lucky Few made the big jump of the century in owning America's
corporations just as they did in so many areas of life including schooling or parenthood or employment rates.

Generations and Pension Coverage

Although the Baby Boom surpasses the Lucky Few in corporate investment if we count new defined-contribution retirement plans invested in stocks, limiting our attention only to defined-contribution
retirement plans misses a complementary aspect of the picture. While

Baby Boomers are opting in greater numbers than ever before for such defined-contribution plans, in many cases this has happened because a different alternative that was available to the Lucky Few and other older generations has been disappearing like a rug pulled out from beneath the feet of the Baby Boomers and Generation X (Bloom & Freeman 1992).

The older alternative to the defined-contribution retirement plan, the defined-benefit or traditional "pension" plan, may be on the road to extinction in the twenty-first century. When people in earlier generations participated in employer-sponsored pension plans, normally they and/or their employers (the details of contributions involved a dizzying complexity) contributed money on a regular basis to a pension fund maintained and invested by the employer, acting on behalf of the employees.

These contributions were *not* employee purchases of shares of stock in any corporation – employees didn't own anything except a contracted right to a pension from the employer. If the employer could make more money from investing the pension fund than had been contracted as benefits promised to employees, the additional profit belonged to the employer, not the employees. On the other hand, if the employer promised more in benefits than could be made by investing the pension fund, the company was still liable to pay the benefits. If an employer went out of business, employees had to stand in line with other creditors if they expected fulfillment of their pension contracts. While employees with these original-format pension plans sometimes got reports about how much money they had contributed over the years, the actual contract between the employee and the company specified pension payments as "defined benefits." Typically, a formula determined this benefit based on total years of service and some kind of averaging of a certain number of previous years of income, in much the same way that Social Security benefits still are calculated at this writing.

This formula had only the vaguest relation to the total amount of money the employee had paid into the pension fund. Since they were not direct investments in corporations, these traditional pension plans don't get counted in any measure used when people talk about investing in the corporate world. The employees had rights to pensions, but their employers (or their unions) were the ones investing the money and making any profits.

Thus the fact that Baby Boomer men in 2001 had more investments in corporate stocks than did Lucky Few men in 1983 is offset by the fact that Baby Boomers have had fewer opportunities to participate in traditional pension plans. When the Census Bureau's Current Population Surveys asked people whether they participated in any kind of pension plan at all (either defined-benefit or defined-contribution), a similar 60 percent of Lucky Few men in the 1983 CPS and 60 percent of Baby Boomer men in the 2001 CPS reported participation in such plans. The difference was that the Lucky Few more often had defined-benefit plans (which we should count as a retirement resource *in addition* to their personal stock investments) while the Baby Boomers more often had defined-contribution plans (which get counted directly as *part* of their personal stock investments).

Whether we consider gains in employment itself, advances in occupational standing, traditional pension-plan coverage, or stock investments in corporate America, the Lucky Few emerge as probably the financially luckiest generation of the twentieth century. Counting both what they earned and what they kept, the success of the Lucky Few men paradoxically "allowed" Lucky Few women to lag behind in generational terms in education and economic performance. The economic success of the Lucky Few also encouraged comparatively early marriages and the reproductive renaissance we know as the Baby Boom. It is true that the Lucky Few experienced a drop in union membership compared to the Good Warriors, but that is hardly a misfortune when we remember that it resulted chiefly from the Lucky Few's shift away from blue-collar employment to corporate business positions, management and the professions.

Having established the unparalleled success of the Lucky Few in their adult economic roles, we turn in the next chapter to a more subjective side of generational patterns: the question of public opinion and differences in attitudes about major issues.

Chapter 7
At the Heart of the Silent Majority

Contents

Maturation or Generations

Attitudes about morality, politics and related issues may change over time for individuals as part of the normal process of maturation and aging (Glenn & Grimes 1968, Glenn 1973). Winston Churchill summed up this maturation-and-aging perspective when he remarked, "If you're not a liberal at twenty, you have no heart, and if you're not a conservative at forty, you have no head." American poet Robert Frost acknowledged this same idea when he said he never dared to be radical when young for fear it would make him conservative when old.

On the other hand, Strauss and Howe (1991) assume that different generations, growing up in different historical epochs, develop contrasting attitudes (and even personality types) that persist throughout their lifetimes – one of the bedrock assumptions underlying the framework of their book. Kingsley Davis (1940) similarly pointed out that differences in outlook between generations become particularly important in times of rapid change.

Maturational versus generational perspectives may not inherently contradict each other, but they frequently offer conflicting explanations of everyday facts – the maturational perspective would explain an older person's conservatism as a gradual process of change in attitudes with advancing age, while the generational perspective might suggest that the person always had been more conservative as a result of growing up in more conservative times in the past. A younger generation with more conservative opinions than their elders would be difficult for this maturational perspective to explain, but not for the generational perspective.

If we consider social classes rather than generations, Oscar Lewis is famous for suggesting (1966) that no matter where you find chronic poverty in the world (whether in rural Ireland, villages of Mexico, or in the American South) the life experience that comes from poverty tends to produce similar mentalities. This "culture of poverty" argument predicts that people caught in inherited poverty will tend to have a present-time orientation (as opposed to long-term planning for the future), sharply differentiated sex roles in which men spend time with friends while women spend time with relatives, and so on. The culture of poverty perspective posits stable, persistent patterns of attitude and personality shaped by social class, somewhat as Strauss and Howe characterize generational contexts.

On the other hand, in the same way that the maturation-and-aging perspective downplays the permanence of attitudes for any generation, the debate about psychological effects of poverty led other scientists like Elliot Liebow to argue against the culture of poverty. The homeless men he studied in *Tally's Corner* (1967) had hopes, dreams, fears, likes and dislikes – in short, most attitudes – very much like those of middle-class suburban families. Liebow stressed that the very different behavior of these men sprang not from distinctive (some might say "deviant") personalities or attitudes, but simply from the very different material context in which they found themselves living–and he implied that if this context changed again, so might the men's behavior.

Liebow's side of this debate also triumphs at the end of the motion picture *Trading Places*, in which a rich, pampered Dan Akroyd and an unfortunate but clever Eddie Murphy find themselves hijacked and transplanted by the wealthy, arrogant Duke brothers into each other's material worlds. Akroyd and Murphy eventually team up at the film's end to outwit the Dukes (played by Hard Timers Don Ameche and Ralph Bellamy) with the help of fellow Baby Boomer Jamie Lee Curtis, and make their own fortunes in the process. From start to finish, the film depends on the fundamental attitudes and values shared by Akroyd and Murphy despite the material gulf that separated their initial worlds.

The debate about the culture of poverty has obvious implications for understanding our historical generations. We already know that behaviour varied tremendously across these seven generations. Given the effects of war, economic depression and expansion, large and small generations, and other historical influences shown in earlier chapters, we might view generational differences in marriage timing, enlistment in the military, parenthood, timing of retirement and the like the way Liebow did – as products of sharply different material contexts of everyday life. However, the question still remains: did contrasts in life experiences also transform beliefs and attitudes in each generation in distinctive ways? For example, do members of Generation X (as many popular books on management techniques suggest) need a steady stream of recognition and praise, unlike Baby Boomers or the Lucky Few? Do our generations look at the world differently, or do all the generations share the same fundamental attitudes? This chapter offers some evidence on that point.

Measuring Attitudes of the Generations

Research has assembled a substantial body of findings suggesting there are indeed political generations, though nothing so mathematically precise or magically consistent as the uniform fifteen-year generations proposed by Jose Ortega y Gasset (see footnotes to Chapter 1). One of the earliest examples of political research stressing stable generational patterns in public opinion (Evan 1959) pointed the way to using survey data to study these issues, with special emphasis on political beliefs and voting patterns. The quarter-century that followed Evan's paper became the heyday of research on generational politics, with some scholars (Rintala 1963, Flacks 1967, Cutler 1968 & 1976, Klecka 1971, Thomas 1974, Bengston 1975,

DeMartini 1985, Billingsley & Tucker 1987) championing the generational perspective. Billingsley and Tucker even define generations that fairly closely match those identified by Strauss and Howe (see Chapter 2) or in this book. Klecka (1971) and others found that political attitudes change less within generations over time, and more within specific age groups as different generations pass through them.

Vital statistics and census data at the heart of our study so far are silent on what people think and feel. For detailed study of what our generations believe, we must turn to national opinion surveys. Fortunately, for many years the National Opinion Research Center has compiled the results of a general-purpose survey known as the General Social Survey (GSS), asking a scientific sample of Americans hundreds of questions covering almost every imaginable subject. We can sort the answers by sex, age (and therefore generation), and other background characteristics as desired. The results of these surveys, conducted nearly every year for more than three decades, are available at web site www.icpsr.umich.edu/GSS/, where users can replicate results presented here or even go on to make investigations of their own. The variable in each survey called "COHORT," representing the year of birth of each respondent, enables us to group people with the same birth years together into the seven historical generations identified at the start of Chapter 2.

When looking for age or generational patterns in GSS results, social scientists typically construct complex statistical models to filter out differences in education, urban versus rural residence, and perhaps such things as marital status or occupation. Such models attempt to measure how much of observed opinion differences remain as a separate residual effect of belonging to one generation or another. We do *not* introduce such "controls" here, though we already know that our historical generations differ sharply in terms of education and other background experiences. We want to consider the actual opinions of each generation *as it is*, incorporating any indirect effects of these other factors. After all, no one can go back and remove years of education from people in one generation and redistribute this schooling to another generation. Each generation's background has become a part of who its members are, and precisely that full reality of each generation, incorporating these accumulated differences, is what interests us here. No matter where these differences come from, the point for us is that they do exist.

In many ways, our historical generations do show differences in how they feel about major issues in American life. These differences tend to persist over time, consistent with what other scholars have noted. While each generation undergoes the "Churchill effect" while growing older, certain generational differences do seem to persist independent of any pure aging or maturational effect. All of the questions and issues considered here were posed repeatedly over the long time span covered by the General Social Surveys, so answers from each generation average out any unusual responses that might appear in one particular year.

Gradual Shifts in Opinion

While generations reveal many persistent differences of opinion, some of these differences follow gradual, rather unremarkable patterns of variation. For example, Fig. 7.1 shows responses to a pair of questions about attitudes toward married women working outside the home.

One question asked respondents whether they agreed or disagreed with the following statement: "A working mother can establish just as warm and secure a relationship with her children as a mother who does not work." The bars in the left half of the figure show responses of men and women in each generation. Women agree with the statement more than men in every generation. Only a minority of Hard Timers agreed, but each new generation agreed with the statement more, resulting in a strong majority of agreement for both sexes in Generation X.

Similarly, the bars on the right side of the figure for each generation of men and women show percentages of respondents who "...approve or disapprove of a married woman earning money in business or industry if she has a husband capable of supporting her." Both men and women again show a gradual increase in approval of working wives from one generation to the next, with women ahead of men in this regard in every generation.

This kind of pattern does not delineate particular boundaries between our generations. Probably the same gradual increase in tolerance would be visible from one annual birth cohort to another, even within the generations. Such a pattern does not show off our concept of generations in its best light!

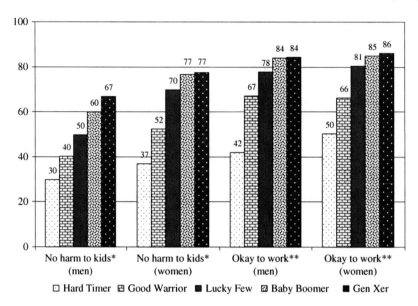

Fig. 7.1 Approve women working outside the home by generation and sex
Source: Original tabulations from the Cumulative General Social Surveys
(ICPSR website).
*"Please tell me whether you strongly agree, agree, disagree, or strongly
disagree with the statement: A working mother can establish just as warm
and secure a relationship with her children as a mother who does not work."
(No harm = agree + strongly agree)
**"Do you approve or disapprove of a married woman earning money
in business or industry if she has a husband capable of supporting her?"
(Okay = approve)

Another much-cited group of attitudes shows similar gradual patterns of change, though not quite so simple as those involving jobs
for women. These are the so-called "institutional" questions, asking
respondents whether they have a great deal of confidence, some confidence, a little confidence, or no confidence at all in some of the major institutional structures of American society. Respondents declare
how they feel about the federal government, big corporations, labor
unions, the press, the clergy representing organized religion, and even
the army. Figure 7.2 shows generational patterns in these "confidence
in institutions" measures for our generations, this time only reporting
results for men because results for women or for both sexes together

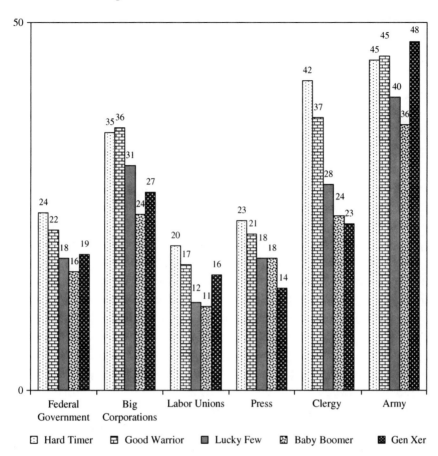

Fig. 7.2 Great confidence in institutions, men by generation
Source: Original tabulations from the Cumulative General Social Surveys
(ICPSR website).

would give almost identical results. These questions do not distinguish
men from women in important ways.

Over the long-term, these measures show declining confidence by
each new generation with respect to key social institutions in American life. Many writers have noticed this trend before, and have talked
about fading civic engagement (see *Bowling Alone* by Robert Putnam
(2000), for example) and other similar ideas. For most of these institutions, the drop in confidence registered by the Lucky Few shows
up as the biggest decline over previous levels reported by any generation of the century. This pattern holds for confidence in the federal

government, in labor unions, in religion and the clergy, and in the army. The Lucky Few's loss of confidence in big corporations rivals the further drop reported among Baby Boomers, and only Generation X lost more confidence than the Lucky Few in journalists and the press.

Why should confidence in institutions drop so much for the Lucky Few, who enjoyed the most rewards from these very institutions and from life in mid-century America in general? Loss of confidence in labor unions makes some sense given this generation's gradual exodus from such organizations, but the parallel loss of confidence in corporations flies in the face of their numerous careers in corporate America. While their success might have made the Lucky Few particularly appreciative of American institutions, perhaps people generally tend to view their successes in life as their own achievements, rather than thinking in terms of the social context that made their success possible (including the advantages of being part of a small generation). Added to this natural tendency of people, we also should recall that Lucky Few men made the largest single jump in educational attainment of any generation, and GSS results show that confidence in institutions is strongest in every generation for people with the least education. People with more education, paradoxically, may be more prone to attribute that success to their own personal efforts rather than to underlying social contexts. We might even say that more educated people have been more fully indoctrinated into the fundamental American cult of individualism.

With less confidence in the framework of the country than earlier generations but more confidence than the Baby Boomers who followed them, the Lucky Few always fall just in the middle of the pack. The "twist" in Fig. 7.2 does not involve the Lucky Few, but instead shows us a surprise about the supposedly disaffected and cynical Generation X. According to their responses in the General Social Survey, members of Generation X do indeed continue the decline in confidence regarding journalists (the press) and the clergy (organized religion), but despite their high levels of education they actually express renewed confidence in several major institutions – the federal government, big business, labor unions, and the army. Since we are concentrating on the Lucky Few as the central theme of this study, we will not go chasing this interesting result, but someone certainly should!

The Abortion Debate

When people discuss public opinion research, one of the hottest issues always involves the thorny, intense and sometimes dangerous debate about induced abortion in the United States. Few public issues generate so much heat and so little light as this debate. Figure 7.3 shows generational responses to a whole battery of survey questions, asking about circumstances in which people would favor or oppose a woman's right to an induced abortion. The questions range from one that raises the least opposition (when the woman's health is in danger) through questions about abortion in case of rape, abortion if

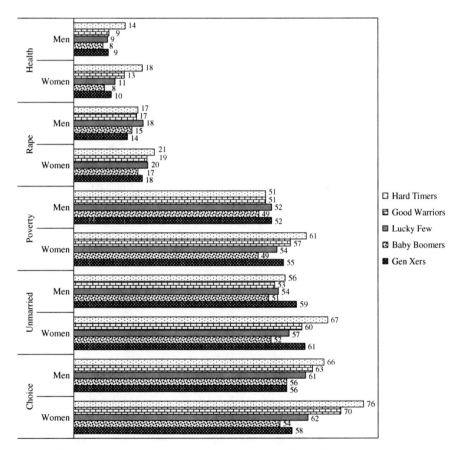

Fig. 7.3 Reasons to oppose abortion by generation and sex
Source: Original tabulations from the Cumulative General Social Surveys (ICPSR website).

the woman is poor and feels unable to provide for the child, abortion if
the woman is unmarried, and ending with the question that raises the
most opposition – when the woman simply desires the abortion for
any personal, unspecified reason. This figure shows the percentage of
men and women in each generation who have said over the years that
they oppose the right to an abortion for each of these reasons.

The figure shows a sharp break between two classes of questions
about abortion – on the one hand, the overwhelming majority of
Americans in all generations would not oppose an induced abortion
when the pregnancy threatens the woman's health or results from rape.
The Hard Timers express the most opposition, but even for them this
amounts to a very small minority of the generation. Opposition falls
for each younger generation until the Baby Boomers show the least
opposition of any generation, but Generation X appears to be slightly
more opposed to abortion than the Baby Boomers, again reversing the
trend observed up to that time across generations.

On the other hand, questions that involve some social reason for the
abortion (or no specified reason at all – the bottom bars in the figure)
bring out much more opposition in all generations. Not only are older
generations more opposed to these social reasons for abortion, but
among them, women oppose socially-justified abortions significantly
more than men do. The stronger opposition of women born at the start
of the century gradually fades away as we move to newer generations,
so that already by the time we look at the Lucky Few most of this
contrast between men and women has disappeared.

Once again, the Lucky Few again appear in Fig. 7.3 in the middle of
the pack on all the abortion questions, somewhere between the higher
opposition of the oldest generations we consider, and the lowest opposition always found among the Baby Boomers.

Social Trust

Not all attitude questions show such smooth, gradual trends, however.
In some cases, responses for earlier generations reveal a rather stable
pattern over time, with little change across generations. Then for later
generations, attitudes that had been stable and fairly constant begin
to change. When this happens, in several important areas of public attitudes the Lucky Few prove to be the last "stable" generation,

with attitudes closely matching those of the Hard Timers and Good Warriors. The changes begin to appear among the Baby Boomers, and often accelerate among the members of Generation X.

For example, several important questions try to tap whether people feel that they truly "belong" to American society, whether they genuinely feel connected to other people, part of something worth their commitment and loyalty. Without this social cement, these feelings that we are all on the same team, many important dimensions of living together can become problematic. Without social trust and a sense of belonging, people give less to charities, ignore strangers in need, cheat more on their taxes, run red lights, and generally lose out on advantages that teamwork can produce in life.

Two particularly powerful questions about social trust, covered in nearly every General Social Survey, ask (1) whether you think that other people act fairly and honestly in their dealings with you and others generally, or rather are opportunistic and willing to cheat you and anyone else whenever they get the chance, and (2) whether you think that other people are willing to be helpful to you when you need it, or are likely to ignore your problems and look out only for themselves.

Each generation's answers over the years appear in Fig. 7.4. The Lucky Few look very much like the Hard Timers and Good Warriors in answers to both questions. For all three of these older generations, less than one-third of respondents gave the cynical answers that people are only out for themselves, and that they will cheat you whenever they get a chance.

However, the share of Baby Boomers giving these cynical answers to the questions jumped to nearly half of all respondents. For Generation X, the cynical answers became the majority opinion for the first time in any generation. What are we to make of this? The increase in personal cynicism for Baby Boomers might fit to some extent with their lower confidence in major public institutions including politics, religion, corporations, unions or the press, but the even greater cynicism about other people for Generation X looks strange when we recall that they also expressed renewed confidence in some major institutions. Can we have faith in the large-scale institutional structures of social life, and yet fundamentally distrust the individual people we meet and deal with on a daily basis? Perhaps people in Generation X want strong institutions to keep all those bad people in line. These questions bear further investigation.

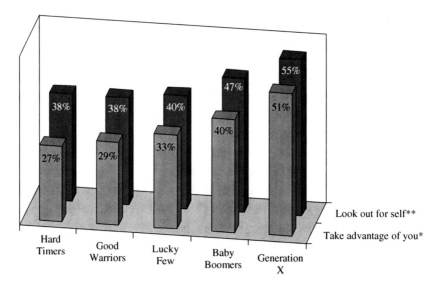

Fig. 7.4 Social trust by generations (both sexes combined)
Source: Original calculations from General Social Surveys.
* "Do you think most people would try to take advantage of you if they got a chance, or would they try to be fair?"
** "Would you say that most of the time people try to be helpful, or that they are mostly just looking out for themselves?"

Newspapers

Media revolutions have transformed our lives repeatedly during the twentieth century, replacing newspapers with radios, radios with televisions, and now televisions with the internet, mobile phones, and other interactive media. According to the GSS, generations up through the Lucky Few relied on newspapers as one of their most salient sources of news and information, and uniformly reported in large numbers that they read a newspaper *every day* (usually as subscribers receiving the paper in their homes).

Figure 7.5 shows that once again, as in the questions about public trust, the Lucky Few represent the last generation in a previously stable pattern of behavior and attitudes. They form the last generation in which over half of all Americans consult an actual newspaper (the physical object made of paper, rather than internet web pages with newspaper stories) every day. The Baby Boomers have fallen below the one-third mark for such readership, and less than a quarter of

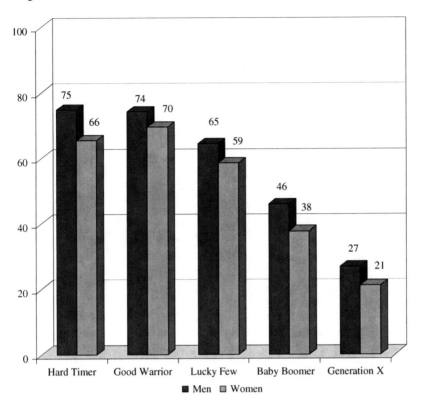

Fig. 7.5 Read newspaper every day
Source: Original tabulations from the Cumulative General Social Surveys (ICPSR website).

Generation X reads a "paper" newspaper daily. These younger generations get most of their news from other sources. The Lucky Few mark the end of a media era.

Busing

Alhough most issues related to race and ethnic identity will be taken up later in Chapter 8, one GSS survey question about these issues further reinforces the picture of the Lucky Few as the last generation to be part of a stable pattern of attitudes, with sharp social changes following among Baby Boomers and Generation X. The GSS survey respondents were asked, "In general, do you favor or oppose the

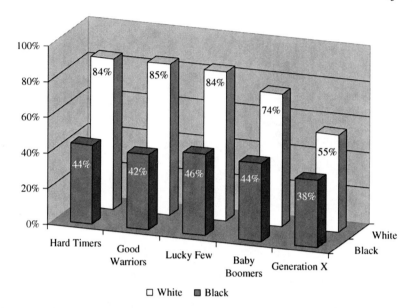

Fig. 7.6 Oppose busing school children (both sexes combined)
Source: Original tabulations from the Cumulative General Social Surveys
(ICPSR website).

busing of (Negro/Black/African–American) and white school children
from one school district to another?"

As shown in Fig. 7.6, attitudes about busing show the same generational pattern for both women and men as for the social trust questions
or for newspaper readership – a stable (and high) level of opposition to
busing among the Hard Timers, Good Warriors and Lucky Few alike,
and then suddenly increased tolerance for busing policies among Baby
Boomers and even more tolerance among members of Generation X.

Firearms

The Lucky Few stand out even more clearly as a generation unto themselves on the ideology of firearms and the debate about gun ownership
and use. The Lucky Few (particularly Lucky Few *women* compared to
other women) are more likely than any other generation of the century
to own their own guns and keep them at home, in their cars, or perhaps
on their person, as shown in Fig. 7.7 (in the rows marked "own gun").
Despite the fact (or perhaps related to the fact) that the Hard Timers

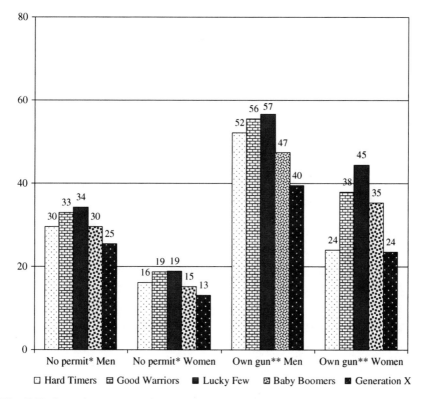

Fig. 7.7 Oppose gun permits and own guns
Source: Original tabulations from the Cumulative General Social Surveys (ICPSR website).
* "Would you favor or oppose a law which would require a person to obtain a police permit before he or she could buy a gun?"
** "Do you happen to have in your home (IF HOUSE: or garage) any guns or revolvers?"

and Good Warriors actually experienced higher risks of combat casualties in wartime, the Lucky Few have turned out to be the gun-owning champions of the century.

The GSS also asked whether people should be required to obtain government permits for guns they own. As shown in Fig. 7.7, the Lucky Few expressed more opposition to this idea of gun permits than any other generation. This ideological issue goes well beyond familiarity with guns, fondness for hunting or target-shooting, or even issues of personal security. The share of people in each generation who oppose gun licenses is much smaller than the share who actually own guns, so clearly many gun owners have no objection to this idea. The opposition to licensing firearms taps into ideological concerns over constitutional rights and freedoms, and leads us to another related sense in which the Lucky Few stand out from our other generations.

Political Parties

Although the modern party competition between Democrats and Republicans sometimes has been complicated by non-party candidates and even small organized third political parties, these two gigantic groups continue to dominate politics in the United States. They receive nearly all campaign contributions and include nearly all major office-holders at the state and federal level. The journalistic short-hand of "red" states and "blue" states in discussions of recent elections refers in large measure to this balance between Republicans (red) and Democrats (blue), but journalists and other pundits also routinely use the red/blue distinction to discuss a whole constellation of other political values and opinions, and sometimes to attach these to one party or the other. "Red states" not only represent places where the Republican party dominates the electoral process, but also places where generally conservative political positions and values are believed to be more prevalent.

Equating the Republican party with conservative politics and the Democratic party with liberal political positions, however, is an oversimplification. The equation breaks down, in particular, when we try to apply it across our American generations of the twentieth century (Converse 1976).

First, consider how each of our generations identifies with our two major political parties. Figure 7.8 aggregates the reported party identification of GSS respondents over the past three decades of survey results, grouping them by generation. The Hard Timers and Good Warriors both show clear, long-term political effects of their experience with the Great Depression and the policies of Frankin D. Roosevelt's Democratic administration. Many people who lived through that period credited Roosevelt with rescuing the country from a terrible economic mess they identified with Herbert Hoover and the Republicans. FDR's administration also led the country during the Good War, so patriotic loyalty combined with economic judge-

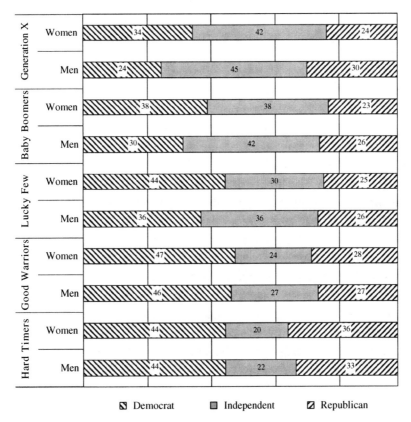

Fig. 7.8 Political party identification by generation and sex
Source: Original tabulations from the Cumulative General Social Surveys
(ICPSR website).

ments to make nearly half of all Hard Timers (both men and women)
identify with the Democratic party on a rather permanent basis. The
Good Warriors have seen themselves even more as Democrats than
the Hard Timers. This party loyalty is still visible in Fig. 7.8 in the
striped segments at the left side of the bars for these early generations.

Nearly half of the Lucky Few also identify themselves as Democrats,
particularly Lucky Few women. (The "Democrat" category in Fig. 7.6
combines two survey responses, "strong" and "weak" Democrats.)
For men, however, a retreat from the Democrats began among the
Lucky Few and then continued for Baby Boomer men. By the time we
get to Generation X, less than one-fourth of men identify themselves

as Democrats. This retreat from the Democrats also appears among women, but they seem to lag about two generations behind the men in this trend.

While one might think that this would be good news for the Republican party, in fact that is not the case. More than one-third of Hard Timers and Good Warriors identify themselves as Republicans (also combining two survey responses, "strong" and "weak" Republican identification), but just as younger generations identify less with Democrats, they also identify less with Republicans. Only about a third of the Lucky Few declare themselves to be Republicans, depicted as the striped segments on the right side of the bars in the figure. The Baby Boomers, both men and women, retreated even more than the Lucky Few from calling themselves Republicans. Only Generation X (again echoing other trends noted for them above) show small signs of returning to Republican party identification.

Thus there has been a general retreat from unconditional identification with *both* major political parties. Reasons for this are hotly debated among political scientists, but one plausible explanation might be that both the parties have fallen more and more into the hands of activist cadres with increasingly narrow special-issue agendas. These party insiders with extreme views may have left behind the great middle mass of American voters, who must now be courted frantically with barrages of advertising in order to induce at least some of them to vote at election time.

Such an interpretation fits well with the third piece of the puzzle in Fig. 7.8 – the steady expansion of the share of both men and women in each generation who identify themselves as Independents, uncommitted to either political party in the absence of any specific candidate or issue. The "Independent" category, shown as the shaded middle segments of the bars in the Figure, combines "independent near republican" with plain vanilla "independent" and "independent near democrat."

Liberal, Moderate or Conservative

To confirm that the drift away from both political parties probably stems from the actions of party elites rather than representing some more fundamental shift in attitudes among voters, we turn to the other side of this coin, shown in Fig. 7.9. While identification with the major political parties has waned, the same cannot be said about underlying ideological or political attitudes. Figure 7.9 displays General Social Survey responses to a very different question, asking people not which political party they support, but whether they see themselves as liberals, moderates, or conservatives. As for party identification above, we have collapsed some categories of possible answers. For example, what the left-hand segments of the bars in Fig. 7.9 show as "Liberal" combines three possible survey answers: "extremely liberal", "liberal", and "slightly liberal." Conservatism also collapses three equivalent categories into one, but "Moderate" was a single category with a very large number of responses in the original surveys, and has not been combined with anything else here.

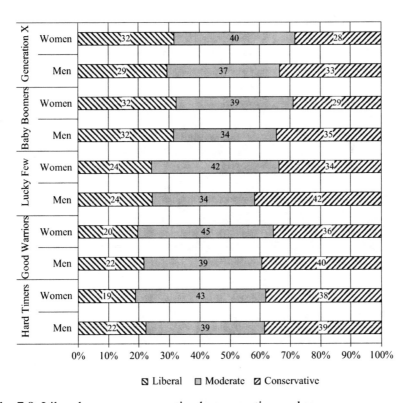

Fig. 7.9 Liberal versus conservative by generation and sex
Source: Original tabulations from the Cumulative General Social Surveys (ICPSR website).

About twice as many of the Hard Timers and Good Warriors saw themselves as conservatives as those who said they were liberals – roughly forty percent conservative to twenty percent liberal. For Baby Boomers and Generation X these categories (liberal, moderate, and conservative) divide the population into roughly equal groups. Those who call themselves moderates include about forty percent of every generation, so the expansion of liberalism in younger generations came at the expense of conservatism.

These patterns in Fig. 7.9 look strange when compared to generational shifts in party identification, already seen in Fig. 7.8. A decline in conservative identification might make sense when matched with the decline in identification with the Republican party across generations. But the increase in liberal identification looks particularly strange when compared to the even faster retreat of younger generations from the Democratic party. What is going on here?

To answer that question in detail, Fig. 7.10 risks overloading the reader with a lot of information, in order to display a truly fascinating underlying pattern. This Figure shows a separate pie chart for each political party grouping within each generation – Hard Timer

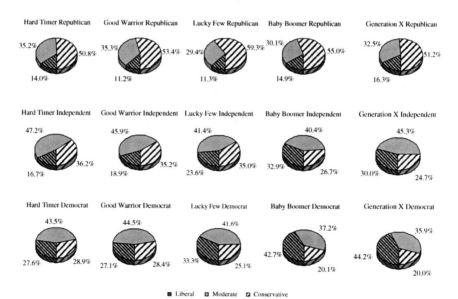

Fig. 7.10 Party identification and political views by generation
Source: Original tabulations from the Cumulative General Social Surveys (ICPSR website).

Democrats, Lucky Few Republicans, Baby Boomer Independents, and every other possible combination of generations and party identification. Each pie chart shows the division of that category of people among liberals, moderates, and conservatives.

Looking across the rows for Republicans or Democrats shows the generational trends in liberalism or conservatism within that political party. Looking down the columns for each generation compares the political segments of the generation. All the details are there. The difficult part, with so much information, then involves finding the most important patterns.

Starting with the party faithful, Democrats have polarized politically as they have contracted to a smaller and smaller fraction of each generation. Only a little over one-fourth of Hard Timer or Good Warrior Democrats call themselves liberal. In fact, conservatives actually outnumber liberals among Democrats from these earlier generations. These are the Democrats who remember FDR, the Good War, and growing up in the Great Depression.

Newer generations of Democrats are less likely to call themselves conservative, and much more likely to call themselves liberals. They remember the Civil Rights movement, the Vietnam War, and other facets of a very different historical period. In fact, liberal identification has crowded out both conservatives and moderates among younger generations of self-identified Democrats. This fits with both Fig. 7.8 on party identification and Fig. 7.9 comparing liberals and conservatives.

Republicans always have been more politically polarized and homogenous than the Democrats or Independents. In every generation, more than half of all Republicans identified themselves as conservatives, compared to somewhere between one-third and one-fourth of the Democrats and Independents. On the other hand, a very small share (between one-sixth and one-eighth) of Republicans in every generation would describe themselves as liberals. As declared Republicans shrank to a smaller and smaller share of each new generation, they also became more ideologically polarized.

The Lucky Few, in fact, emerge as the most conservative Republicans of any generation in the twentieth century. Nearly sixty percent of Lucky Few Republicans say they are conservatives and only about ten percent claimed to be liberals. Moderate Republicans also are scarcer among the Lucky Few than in any other generation. The Lucky Few are at the heart of that brand of Republican (and Democratic) politics that stresses the ideological aspect of party identification and special-issue politics geared to mobilizing core voters for the party (the so-called "base"), a political approach that has been so prominent in the opening years of the new 21st century. It will be interesting to see how both political parties change as leadership roles inevitably pass down to Baby Boomers and members of Generation X in coming decades.

Finally we turn to the Independents in the middle row of the figure. This group expanded in each new generation, at the expense of both political parties. Just under half (always between 40 and 50 percent) of the Independent voters in every generation also call themselves ideological Moderates. The other half of all Independents split between liberals and conservatives. Conservatives outnumber liberals by two-to-one among Hard Timer and Good Warrior Independents, but liberals actually outnumber conservatives among both Baby Boomer and Generation X Independents. The Lucky Few Independents provide the transition or "tipping point" between these two contrasting patterns for older and younger generations.

In many ways, then, not the least being political identity (but also including public opinion issues ranging from public trust to gun control or abortion) the Lucky Few and our other generations emerge from this chapter as distinctive groups in some important ways. Just as generations differed when considering the details of their family lives, economic triumphs and frustrations, or military service, the Lucky Few, Good Warriors and Baby Boomers differ when it comes to many of these matters of conscience and belief.

What can we conclude about the debates noted at the start of this chapter? Do changes in social context fundamentally modify attitudes and personalities (in this case for generations), or do such changes in context merely produce different behavioral reactions while attitudes and personalities remain essentially stable and consistent for generations? A few GSS questions about political identity and public trust certainly can't resolve such a complex issue conclusively. We have seen some evidence that key attitudes have indeed shifted across generations, but not in ways that we can clearly identify with the historical context that shaped each generation. For example, we are left with the puzzling paradox that members of Generation X, despite their high levels of schooling, display new-found trust in many basic social institutions. They also express renewed opposition to abortion and identification with conservatism and the Republican party. Yet these same Generation X members also show record levels of *lack* of trust in the other people they meet in everyday life. The Lucky Few, despite their unparallelled successes, showed the biggest drop from the generation before them in the same measure of trust in basic social institutions. The Lucky Few also displayed an unparalleled love for firearms that is hard to explain in terms of the historical context that shaped their generation. Despite dramatic changes they experienced in schooling, marriage timing, parenthood, careers and the like, as a generation the Lucky Few often exhibit a "solidarity" with the earlier Hard Timer and Good Warrior generations that supports the idea of stable, consistent attitudes across generations in spite of dramatic structural social change.

In short, despite several interesting variations in attitudes across our seven generations, it seems too strong to call these "fundamental shifts." Further, it is difficult to pinpoint specific features shaping different generations that might be responsible for the trends. Thus one might read these results from the point of view of either side in the ongoing debate between maturation and generations. Either way, however, in subjective as well as objective terms, the concept of generations provides a valuable tool for gaining deeper understanding of the American scene.

Chapter 8
The Lucky Few in Black and White

Contents

Nativity, National Origins and Race

Americans underwent a fascinating pendulum-swing of self-definition during the twentieth century. A country of several hundred million people was bound to invent some ingenious ways to sort itself out into distinctive subgroups, but over the past century the people of the United States revised their fundamental self-image not once but twice.

The century opened with Americans defining themselves based on their national origins. By mid-century they had shifted to a more simplistic, streamlined concept of "race," mainly focused on black and white. This streamlined concept of race prevailing at mid-century meant that the racial distinctions most important for studying and understanding the Lucky Few involve black-white contrasts, such as those highlighted later in this chapter. Certainly other kinds of

E. Carlson, *The Lucky Few*,
© Springer Science+Business Media B.V. 2008

distinctions existed among the Lucky Few, but these were less salient than in any other generation of the century. Then by the end of the century, America's self-image began to swing back toward the original scheme based on national origins – though with a new twist. These two transformations had everything to do with the passage of our successive generations.

Nativity refers to the distinction between native-born citizens and foreign-born people who enter the country as immigrants. Until the mid-twentieth century, nativity always played a major role in residential patterns, choices of marriage partners, or preferences and prejudices at hiring time, appearing near center stage in the theatre of American social life. In the brief profiles of our seven generations presented in Chapter Two, nativity provided a surprising link between the first generations of the century (the New Worlders and Hard Timers) and the last (Generation X and the New Boomers). At both the start and the end of the 1900s, high tides of immigration yielded large shares of foreign-born people in these generations.

Beyond the simple fact of being born inside or outside the United States, the national origins of immigrants also mattered very much as the twentieth century began. Immigrants tend to congregate in neighborhoods with their own churches, languages, foods, recreation, and even people to be their partners in marriage, business and other walks of life. The flood of immigrants at the beginning of the century was kept at arm's length from native-born society by high social barriers against intermarriage or other intensive contacts.

An inward-looking tendency based on national origins applied as much in the countryside as it did in crowded urban neighborhoods. Garrison Keillor has memorialized the phenomenon of the Norwegian bachelor farmer in the lore of his native Minnesota, but has not explained the origins of this peculiar group to his radio audience. The sad and simple fact was that the daughters of Norwegian immigrants on those lonely Minnesota farms moved away to towns and cities in great numbers as soon as they were able, taking jobs as maids, teachers, and other non-farm occupations and leaving an acute shortage of women in the countryside for young Norwegian men. The young men who stayed on the farms often could find no one of their own national origin group to marry. Rather than marry some "other" sort of woman (Polish, perhaps, or of other national origins) they became the iconic bachelor farmers of Keillor's stories. In my own mother's family, the four sisters all moved away to urban futures. The two brothers both remained behind as Norwegian bachelor farmers.

In the early 1900s, a widespread and well-established consensus interpreted diverse national origins in terms of "race," in the sense that this *biologism* (a concept pretending biological origins, but without rigorous biological scientific content) was understood then. The idea was neither new nor unique to the United States. In 1866 James Hunt, the founder of the Anthropological Society of London, had declared that anthropology's primary truth ". . .is the existence of well-marked psychological and moral distinctions in the different races of men." Odd as it may seem today, people tended to think of the English, French, Italians, Germans and Irish as members of different "races," each with their own unique inborn psychologies as well as physiological traits. For example, the French had a violent revolution in 1789 while the English did not, due to a difference in what was described as "the genius of the race" particular to each group (Le Bon, 1894).

Scientists largely abandoned this essentialist view (treating races as objective biological categories, something like sub-species of humanity) over the course of the twentieth century. No coherent, consistent group of biogenetic traits could be identified that correlate well with perceived races of people. Some scholars who became known as eliminativists, led in particular by Ashley Montagu (1964), wanted to discard the entire concept as a result of such scientific research. However, the concept of race remains alive and extremely healthy in American society right down to the present day. The lack of clear biological foundations for races has generated new understanding of the ways that each society selectively constructs (and therefore modifies over time) its definition of "race" and the categories within it – the constructivist approach (DuBois 1940, Omi & Winant 1994, Smedley 1999) that our consideration of different generations so nicely illustrates.

From National Origins to Black and White

The first swing of the pendulum moved away from emphasizing national origins. Instead of interpreting nativity and/or nationality through the lens of a sort of finely-grained biologistic racialism, national origin boundaries (so crucial for the personal identities of people in the New Worlder and Hard Timer generations) lost a good deal of their salience by mid-century. "Race" got simpler. Although the American population was compartmentalized into nationality groups and further divided between immigrants and native-born, enlightening accounts have recently appeared describing how Jewish (Brodkin 2000), Irish (Ignatiev 1995) and Italian (Salerno & Guglielmo 2003) immigrants all used labor unions, churches and political parties to overcome initial identification of immigrants with "nonwhites" and to become "white" over the course of the twentieth century.

The Census Bureau, responsible for categorizing the people it counts, actually furthered this streamlining of the diversity of everyday life into a few broad race categories. All Europeans counted as "white" in census definitions. In the 1900 Census, 87.8 percent of the population (including all the different European nationality groups) were counted as white, 11.7 percent were black, and half a percent were divided among the other enumerated race categories (mostly Native Americans and Chinese, and mostly in the western states). This uncritical and un-biological categorization of a few official races for the United States was later set in bureaucratic concrete by the Office of Management and Budget (1977a, b) decree that all federal forms and statistics must measure the concept of race using exactly four categories: American Indian or Alaskan Native, Asian or Pacific Islander, Black, or White. (A blank space on census forms and some other documents also allowed people to "write in" other races, an option that became more important at the end of the century as discussed below.) Beyond the official four government-recognized race groups, other distinctions (say, between Irish and Ukrainians) do not exist. People from Afghanistan, India, Malaysia, China and Japan are all lumped together as Asians in the same "race" category, strange though that undoubtedly seems to them.

We do not have to search far for the explanation of this weakening of nationality as a foundation of "racial" identity. The cause was simply a drastic reduction in immigration. For the Lucky Few and the Good Warriors, as already noted in Chapter 2, the tide of immigration ebbed dramatically in mid-century. As a result, hardly any members of the Good Warrior or Lucky Few generations were foreign-born immigrants who had to struggle with adapting to a new country and a whole new way of life, falling back on their communities of national origin for support and comfort (Skrabanek, 1995). About nine of every ten people in these middle generations of the century were born in the United States, grew up listening to the same radio broadcasts, discovered the television age together, attended the same schools, married one another, and served together in large numbers in the military. National origins became less salient simply because nearly everyone actually shared a single national origin – they were native-born Americans. For these mid-century generations (the Good Warriors and the Lucky Few in particular) race became largely a matter of black and white.

Native-born homogeneity does not mean, of course, that the whole idea of ethnic identity disappeared from these generations. The absence of a "rainbow" of race options on census forms did not stop people from thinking of themselves in terms of national origins, and they still enthusiastically answered other census questions about where their ancestors had been born. Italian-Americans like New York Mayor Rudi Giuliani or Mafia don John Gotti, German-Americans like General Norman Schwartzkopf, Japanese-Americans like George Takei (*Star Trek*'s Mr. Sulu), Greek-Americans like Massachusetts Governor Michael Dukakis and a host of other hyphenated Americans with immigrant grandparents or parents still grew up among the Lucky Few with their distinctive cuisines, family celebrations, religious orientations, regional patterns of residence, and all the other features of rich ethnic heritages.

However, the distinction between nativity and ethnic identity is a crucial one. It is one thing to say you are an Italian-American or a Polish-American, but something quite different to say you actually were born and grew up in Italy or Poland before coming to the United States. The large share of foreign-born people among New Worlders and Hard Timers heightened those generations' awareness of nativity and national origins. By mid-century, nativity and nationality faded into the background of the social universe inhabited by Good Warriors and the Lucky Few, and also lost their connection to the concept of race along the way. Everyone became "white," as noted above. This happened not because these generations suddenly become more enlightened and tolerant, but because foreign-born people were much harder to find among their ranks. The old immigration from southern and eastern Europe that dominated the first decades of the twentieth century had been turned off like a faucet. The new immigration from

Latin America and Asia that has made Generation X and the New
Boomers multicultural again had not yet begun.

From Black and White back to National Origins

After the Lucky Few, to some extent among the Baby Boomers but
especially for Generation X and the New Boomers, immigration re-
started as discussed in Chapter 2 above. Along with this rising share
of foreign-born Americans, the return swing of the pendulum began
to gather demographic and social momentum. The powerful tendency
of Americans to think of themselves through the lens of "race" did
not disappear or weaken, but as with the first streamlining of ethnic
identities into a few broad racialized categories, the meaning of race
began to shift again. Unprecedented diverse immigrant streams from
every corner of the world, especially Latin America and Asia, began to
swing the pendulum of constructed racial identity back toward complexity. As the title of Foner and Fredrickson's authoritative edited
volume (2004) on the history of immigration, race and ethnicity in the
United States suggests, today the concept of race is *Not Just Black and
White*.

The Census Bureau, though lagging behind such social currents as
great bureaucracies often do, actually took some tiny steps toward
recognizing the new diversity. They revised the census race question
to allow people to choose more than one category, and split Asians
and Pacific Islanders into separate groups (Office of Management and
Budget 1997). These changes don't amount to much, to be sure, but
they do constitute official recognition that something was going on
in American society. One of the most fascinating examples of the new
redefinition of race in America concerns immigrants and their children
from Latin America, particularly Mexico, but similar patterns appear
for other race/origin groups.

Census forms included an item allowing people to self-identify as
having Spanish surnames from the beginning of the twentieth century, although this item was dropped after the 1980 census. Beginning
in 1930, there was also an item for self-identifying Hispanic origins
(meaning from Latin America, although Portuguese-speaking Brazil
and French-speaking Haiti are not technically Hispanic). These census
questions about ethnicity always have existed completely apart from

questions about race. "Hispanic" has never been a category for the race question on census forms. Those who marked "Hispanic" also had to choose a race, and are recorded as white Hispanics, black Hispanics, or even Asian Hispanics.

However, people in the United States who see themselves as Hispanic increasingly insist that this category should be recognized as a race, possibly because race has become enshrined as a consideration in many Federal budget and policy decisions. Not only do people today check the appropriate Hispanic identity items on census forms, but they choose "other" for the race question and then write in "Hispanic" or some variation on this concept. These actions illustrate deliberate efforts to construct a new race category, an excellent illustration of the constructed nature of the concept itself. The 1980 census actually tabulated this "write-in vote" for a Hispanic race category in published results. The increasing number of people choosing this way of expressing Hispanic identity forms a major part of the resurgence of categories other than black and white appearing in recent census counts, as shown in Fig. 8.1 below.

Also included in this neither-black-nor-white category are increasing numbers of Americans from Asian backgrounds, including immigrants and their families from Vietnam, India, China, Japan, the Philippines, Korea, and other Asian countries. The share counting themselves as neither black nor white is greater in every younger generation after the Good Warriors and Lucky Few, the two predominantly black-or-white generations of the century.

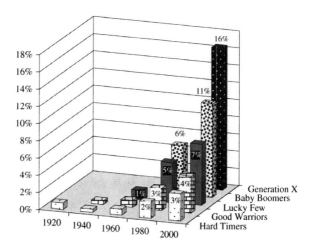

Fig. 8.1 Neither "black" nor "white" Source: Original calculations from Census Public Use Microdata Samples.

But Fig. 8.1 also shows another, even more fascinating tendency – *within* each generation, the share of people counting themselves as something else besides either black or white also has been increasing over time. This remarkable result reflects several trends.

First, immigration of new Americans from Asia and other continents has increased, along with Latin American immigrants who might well be counted as "white" except that many of them seem to be insisting that they do not really want to be. These immigrants, concentrated in the newest generations, do not fit easily into the older simplistic black-white dichotomy.

Second, higher death rates for black Americans and low rates of immigration for groups enumerated as black mean that within each generation, the percentage black erodes as the generation ages. For example, over ten percent of Good Warriors identified themselves as black in 1940, but by 2000 less than eight percent of surviving Good Warriors reported being black.

Third (and most unusual) is clear evidence that some people in each generation *change* self-identification between censuses. For instance, while only 0.34 percent (one-third of one percent) of the Lucky Few claimed to be Native Americans in the 1960 census, by 2000 this share almost doubled to 0.62 percent. This doubling of Native Americans among the Lucky Few could not have been due to immigration, because Native Americans by definition must be native-born. It can not have been due to differential mortality, because Native Americans have much worse survival rates than the white majority of the population (rivalling the mortality experience of black Americans) so they must have been dying off faster than average. The only possible answer is that some people decided, late in the game, to re-identify themselves officially as Native Americans although they had not done so before (Eschbach et al. 1998). The same increase in Native Americans appears in the Baby Boom, where we find 0.76 percent Native Americans in 1980 but 0.81 percent Native Americans by 2000. A similar sort of revision of self-identity goes on among Hispanic Americans when they abandon the "white" category on the race question and begin to check "other" and to write in "Hispanic" in the blank. This tendency to re-identify as other than black or white appears within each generation including the Lucky Few, contributing to this third explanation of the pendulum swing away from the black-or-white dichotomy that dominated considerations of race at mid-century.

The fact that race for the Lucky Few really did boil down largely to black or white, though, actually simplifies consideration of this dimension of the American scene for them. As for all generations, trends, statistics and generalizations made about the Lucky Few in preceding chapters (and in the following chapter about aging and retirement) mostly reflect experiences of white Americans because they form such a large majority of the population. Yet for some fundamental features of life, trends for black members of the Lucky Few generation diverged sharply from those for whites. In some ways the contrast between blacks and whites took different forms in the Lucky Few than in other generations. The remainder of this chapter explores these hidden details of what it meant to be black as well as being part of the Lucky Few.

The Great Migration

The first sharp difference we will examine between black and white Americans concerns a massive population shift in the middle of the twentieth century that has come to be known as the Great Migration (Gregory 2005). As noted above and in earlier chapters, until the United States severely restricted immigration in the mid-1920s, the steady stream of immigrants provided inexpensive workers to fill up the factory districts in huge industrial cities – Akron, Baltimore, Buffalo, Chicago, Detroit, Cleveland, Milwaukee, Newark, Pittsburgh, Toledo, Youngstown and other places. The roll call of these urban industrial engines driven by immigrants still echoes from the turn of the last century, but the new immigration laws suddenly stopped this flow of labor.

Industrialists like Elbert Gary of United States Steel (for whom Gary, Indiana is named) cast their eyes about anxiously, wondering where they would find the continually expanding supply of workers needed in industry. In the end they struck upon a solution – the South. Recruiters in wagons roamed about the southern states, advertising the attractions of great cities with jobs, without the Jim Crow laws of racial segregation (though these cities were segregated just the same) and restrictions on voting and other aspects of life.

Both white and black workers, underemployed in the economies of southern states still stagnating since the end of the Civil War, rushed to the northern industrial cities to fill the vacuum left by the missing immigrants. Mechanization of agriculture and the ecological disaster dubbed the "Dust Bowl" hastened their departures. A disproportionate share of the migrants swarming out of the rural South and into the cities of the Northeast and Midwest were black (Grossman 1989). For example, in 1900 the population of South Carolina was 50 percent black and 50 percent white. By the end of the century, the exodus of the black population combined with arrivals of many white migrants from other states left the state one-third black and two-thirds white. Similar dramatic shifts occurred across most of the South.

Which generations participated in the Great Migration? We can find the answer by comparing people's birthplaces to where they lived at the time of a later census. We consider the 1980 census count, after the Great Migration had happened but before a smaller return-migration trend set in during the final decades of the century. In 1980 the youngest member of the Lucky Few had reached age 35, so we can get a good comparison of the adult relocation of members of both the Lucky Few and the Good Warriors. Baby Boomers also are included for comparison. Although they were younger in 1980, the share of Baby Boomers leaving the South did not change enough between 1980 and 2000 to distort the patterns discussed below.

Generally, about one-third of all people born in any of the eleven Census Divisions[1] appear outside that division in later census counts. Americans move around a lot, more than people in almost any other country. Some may leave when they are young, some may leave when they retire, and some of the young migrants even may return in old age. The "one-third rule" fits for most Census Divisions in most census years.

Black generations living early in the twentieth century were almost entirely born within the Southern region of the country. Thus 91 percent of black Hard Timers, 86 percent of black Good Warriors and 80 percent of black Lucky Few reported Southern states as their birthplaces in the 1980 census. Figure 8.2 concentrates on the three Southern census divisions (South Atlantic, East South Central and West South Central).

The percentages in Figure 8.2 for whites moving away from their birthplaces in Southern census divisions average only 27 percent overall (less than the one-third rule), although even for whites a greater exodus appears for the East South Central division composed

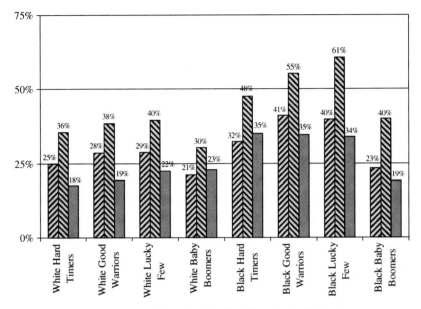

Fig. 8.2 Percent leaving southern divisions by 1980 by division of birth and generation
Source: Original calculations from 1980 Census Public Use Microdata Sample.

of Kentucky, Tennessee, Alabama and Mississippi. By contrast, the taller bars on the right side of Fig. 8.2 show that proportions leaving these same census divisions exceeded the one-third rule for black Americans. Out-migrants averaged nearly half of all black Good Warriors and Lucky Few for the three Southern divisions together, and peaked at nearly *two-thirds* of black Lucky Few from the East South Central divison. Black Good Warriors and Lucky Few spearheaded the Great Migration.

This intensity of migration does not appear among black Baby Boomers. Overall, black Baby Boomers were only about as likely to leave these divisions as were white Boomers, because by the time the Baby Boomers were growing up, the Great Migration had ended. Many of their Good Warrior and Lucky Few parents already had moved away, so less than two-thirds of all black Baby Boomers reported Southern birthplaces in the first place. Only about half of black Americans in Generation X were born in the South. If this trend continues, eventually the share of black Americans born in the South could converge on the 30 percent figure that has been roughly true for every generation of white Americans.

Figure 8.2 tells us nothing about where people went, however. Figure 8.3 below shows destinations for both white and black members of the Lucky Few born in Southern census divisions, who left their birthplaces by 1980. The Appalachian mountain range channelled the Great Migration for black Americans. Those born in the South Atlantic states tended to move to the Northeast (the New England and Middle Atlantic divisions), while those born in East South Central states more often moved to states in the Central region (the East North Central and West North Central divisions) – recently renamed the Midwest region.

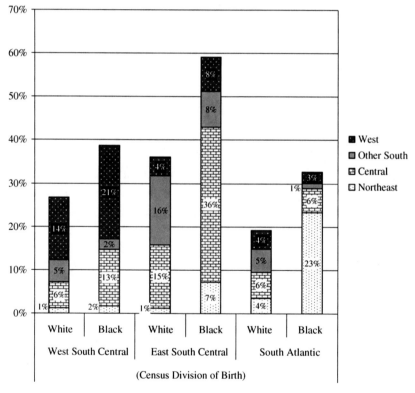

Fig. 8.3 Destinations of black and white lucky few leaving southern census divisions
Source: Original calculations from 1980 Census Public Use Microdata Sample.

The Great Migration, in addition to carrying an enormous population of African-Americans in particular out of the South, also tended to involve rural-to-urban moves. Thus most of the black Lucky Few leaving the South Atlantic states (Florida, Georgia, the Carolinas, Virginia and Maryland) moved to cities like Philadelphia, Newark, New York or Boston. Whites leaving their birthplaces in the South Atlantic, by contrast, were most likely to move to the cities in the Midwest such as Chicago, Detroit, St. Louis, Cincinnati, and so on, or even to move to a different division of the South itself.

Throughout the South, black Lucky Few members were much more likely move away than were whites. This tendency to out-migrate was particularly intense in the East South Central division. The massive exodus of nearly two-thirds of all black Americans born in these states between 1929 and 1945 mostly flowed straight north to great industrial cities like Chicago and Detroit. Again in contrast to the black out-migration, whites leaving the East South Central division were most likely to choose another Southern division as their destination (often cities like Atlanta, Miami, Dallas or Houston). Only a minority of them went north.

The Lucky Few born in West South Central states of Texas, Louisiana, Arkansas and Oklahoma, both black and white, felt the pull of California and other states in the West more strongly since they were closer to the Pacific coast. More of them moved west than in any other direction. The industrial heartland that absorbed most of the Great Migration came in a strong second for people leaving this division, particularly for black migrants.

The Great Migration furnishes another of the great stories that belong to the middle generations of the twentieth century, the Good Warriors and the Lucky Few. Unlike World War II or the Baby Boom, however, the Great Migration only comes into clear focus as part of the life story of these generations when we consider the racial distinctions that divided them between black and white.

Generational Divide in Marriage

We already have seen in Chapter 4 above that the Lucky Few got married much earlier and more universally than for any other generation of the century. Their unparalleled economic success made them the all-time champions of early marriage and parenthood. As with migration patterns, though, looking at the Lucky Few (or any generation) as a whole masks some of the special family life experiences encountered by black Americans. For example, the "marriage boom" involving the Lucky Few barely touched black Americans in that generation.

Consider Fig. 8.4, showing the marital status distributions of each generation by race and sex in early adulthood. A statistical snapshot of each generation comes from a different Census or Current Population Survey year, so each generation can be compared at roughly the same ages – roughly between ages 20 and 40, when most decisions about getting married and having children take place.

Figure 8.4 shows a remarkable acceleration of marriage for white Americans during the first two-thirds of the 1900s, followed by an equally dramatic slowdown after 1970. The Lucky Few have by far the shortest segments for "single" (never married) in the horizontal bars in the Figure. The smaller this segment, the earlier and more universally people married.

Marriage accelerated more for men than for women among both blacks and whites. Women already were marrying earlier than men, so they had less room to marry younger. Greater economic success, based mostly on careers and incomes of men, also helped to account for men's steeper trend toward early marriage.

But the acceleration happened much less among black than among white Americans. Black women experienced only small changes across these generations in the share never married in young adulthood. This lack of an early marriage trend came partly because in early twentieth-century generations (New Worlders and Hard Timers) black women and men both already married earlier than whites. For example, in 1910 young black New Worlder men actually were more married than young white New Worlder men (60 percent versus 53 percent). More black Americans lived in the rural South where everyone tended to marry earlier. Education also ended at younger ages for blacks than for whites.

The other end of the family life cycle (and the other end of the bars in Fig. 8.4) show another dramatic change – the near-disappearance of widows and widowers in midlife as chances of survival increased for all Americans. This improvement also contributed to more young

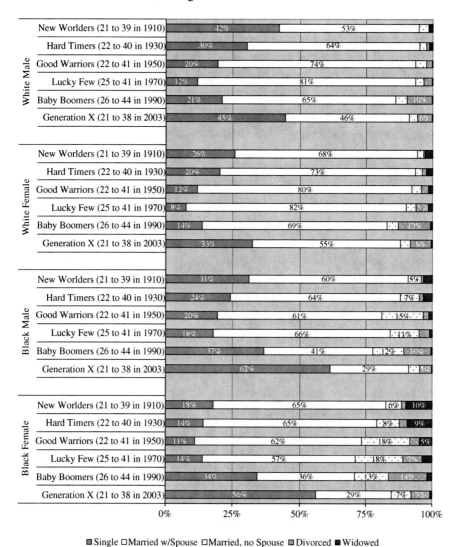

Fig. 8.4 Marriage for generations in young adulthood
Source: Original calculations from Census and Current Population Survey
Public Use Microdata Samples.

adults enumerated as married in each successive generation. Although
mortality only has minor effects on whites at these ages between 20
and 40, higher death rates of black Americans meant that mortality
improvements had a bigger effect on preserving marriages for them.

The effect is particularly strong for successive generations of black women as more of their husbands survived.

For the first four generations of the century, then (from the New Worlders through the Lucky Few) Fig. 8.4 extends to young adults a point made in Chapter 4 about childhood. The Lucky Few not only grew up with both parents more than most generations; they also came closer in young adulthood than any other generation to universal achievement of the ideal of married family life, at least for whites. Over eighty percent of white Lucky Few men and over eighty-one percent of white Lucky Few women were married and living with a spouse when counted at ages 25–41 in the 1970 census, a record unmatched by any other generation.

For black Americans, though, this championship of the Lucky Few looks less clear. Two-thirds of young black Lucky Few men did appear in marriages in that same census, slightly higher than for any other generation of black men. For black women, on the other hand, this two-thirds share counted as young wives living with husbands appeared earlier among the New Worlder and Hard Timer generations. Black Lucky Few women already had begun the slide away from marriage, dropping down to only 57 percent living with husbands. By the time we reach Generation X, only a little over one-fourth of black women between ages 20 and 40 could be found married and living with husbands.

After the Lucky Few, in fact, all the optimistic signs for family life deteriorated very rapidly among both black and white Americans. Although disappearance of married couples living together has been much more dramatic among black than among white Americans, the trend away from marriage is clear for everyone.

The share remaining never-married in the age range between 20 and 40 shot up to more than one-third of black Baby Boomer men, higher than for any previous generation of the century, and then jumped again to almost *two-thirds* of all black men in Generation X – three and one-half times as big a share of men remaining single as had been observed among the Lucky Few only two generations earlier. For black women the postponement/avoidance of marriage was almost as sudden and dramatic. Like black men, over one-third of black Baby Boomer women remained never-married at ages 20–40, and *over half* of black women in Generation X had never married when enumerated in this age range.

These delays for successive black generations far outstripped the parallel trend for whites. Percentages never married in early adulthood had been almost identical for black and white Good Warriors at mid-century (20 percent of men and 12 percent of women, for both blacks and whites). In Generation X at the end of the century the percentage never married for black men and women had risen roughly 50 percent higher than for their white counterparts (62 versus 45 percent for men, and 56 versus 33 percent for women).

Divorce, separation and other spouse absence also increased more for blacks than for whites in each new generation of the century, except for one encouraging sign – all forms of marital disruption appear to have dropped back slightly for Generation X among both blacks and whites. This probably owes something to the fact that Generation X is marrying later than all other generations, among every race and sex group. The later in life that people enter their first marriages, the less likely those marriages are to be disrupted by separation and divorce.

Single Parents and Delayed Marriage

Married life has been caught and "squeezed" between the new delayed marriage trend and the increase in divorce and other marital disruption. The delayed marriage trend grew stronger in each new generation that followed the Lucky Few, as noted above. The tide of separation and divorce, on the other hand, actually rose throughout most of the century. Together, these currents of marital instability produced one of the most serious social problems affecting the United States at the dawn of the twenty-first century – the distressing increase in the extent to which people with money don't have children and people with children don't have money. The economic position of America's children and our social and economic investments in them have been deteriorating along with the family contexts on which they depend (Preston 1984, Morrison 1999).

Single mothers often perform heroic, almost super-human feats to combine parenting with paying jobs, but in the end, one parent simply cannot compete with two – particularly when more and more of those two-parent households have two working spouses. Money and time to invest in children's futures inevitably run short by comparison. Children of elites have never had it so good, but a larger share of children fall between the growing cracks in our social structure with each passing year, and by far the biggest part of the explanation for this distressing trend is exactly the retreat from marriage documented in the previous section.

For a time, in the closing decades of the twentieth century, some pundits and scholars became alarmed about what they called an "epidemic" of teenage childbearing. The fact is, however, that age-specific birth rates among young women, black or white, did not increase in late twentieth-century America. After the Baby Boom ended in the 1960s, rates of teenage childbearing gradually declined. During the Baby Boom in 1960, U.S. vital statistics showed that 89 of every thousand girls between 15 and 19 years old had a baby. In 1970 this rate fell to only 68 births per thousand girls. By 1980 the rate fell to 53, and by 2000 to only 49 births for every thousand girls 15–19 – only about half the rate from 1960. There was no epidemic of births to teen mothers. All the frantic campaigns against teenage motherhood amounted to running alongside a wagon already rolling downhill.

Instead, the retreat from marriage was the real culprit. As marriages for each succeeding generation moved to older ages, marriage delays produced a rapidly-increasing share of young men and women who had never married. Adolescent hormones being what they are, these young adults did not delay sex, pregnancies or childbirth as much as they delayed their marriages. They did delay childbearing somewhat, as can be seen in the birth rates quoted above, but not nearly enough to keep childbearing confined within the rapidly-retreating boundaries of marriages. Dispersion of childbearing outside marriage (Gibson 1976, Carlson 1982) mushroomed, entirely as a result of delayed marriage and in spite of some smaller parallel delays in childbearing. This dispersion has been the taproot of new social problems for America's children.

The delayed marriage trend started by the Baby Boomers and now continuing among Generation X happened much more intensely among black Americans than among whites. Thus the parallel problems affecting children also have been more severe for black families than for white families started in the last decades of the century. Figure 8.5 shows the living arrangements of each generation, separately for white children and black children. The Figure starts with the Good Warriors. (New Worlders and Hard Timers looked very much

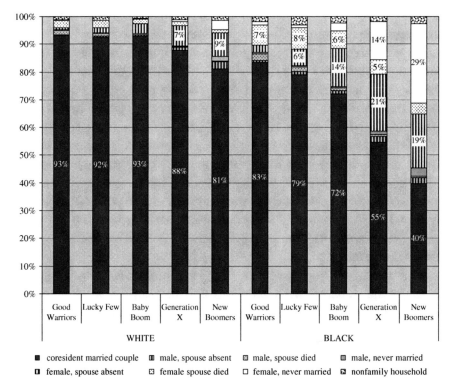

Fig. 8.5 Homes of black and white children before age 10
Source: Original calculations from Census Public Use Microdata Samples.

like the Good Warriors in childhood, except that they were a little
more likely to live with widowed adults.)

The "ideal" category, achieved for most children in the earlier generations, appears as the large bottom segment of each bar in the Figure, showing the share of children under ten who lived with a married
couple when counted by a census. Note, however, that these married
couples are *not* all the actual parents of the children. Some married
couples caring for children could have been grandparents, uncles and
aunts, even sisters or brothers or other relatives and their spouses. The
important thing is that the household included a married couple who
could share the joys and responsibilities, the effort and the financial
expense, of caring for these children in each generation. Fully 93 percent of white Good Warrior children lived in married-couple homes
before age 10, but this living arrangement slipped for each younger
generation. Only 81 percent of white New Boomer children were

counted living with a married couple in childhood. These results parallel the discussion from Chapter 3 above.

The striking feature of this Figure, however, appears when we compare the relatively modest change for white children to the changing experiences of black children across generations. Over 83 percent of black children in the Good Warrior generation lived with married couples, plainly showing that in the early part of the century, family life was almost as stable and supportive for them as for white children. Those black children not living with married couples (again including married-couple grandparents, uncles and aunts, and so on) mostly were living with a widowed household head. This share of children living with widows or widowers declined across generations for both white and black children, as survival improved in American society during the century.

After the Good Warrior generation, both black and white children in following generations lived more and more often in households headed by someone who had lost a spouse through separation or divorce. For the youngest generations, Generation X and especially the New Boomers, the share of children living in homes of single (never-married) adults suddenly exploded as well, driven by the delayed marriage trend just examined above. Particularly for black New Boomer children born after 1982, living with a never-married woman became almost as common as living with any kind of married couple. When we recall how much marriage retreated among young black Americans, this result seems obvious and even inevitable, but it has made life more difficult for these children and also for the adults who care for them.

A Great Educational Leap Forward

Given the serious consequences of dramatic marriage delays in America at the end of the twentieth century, much research attention has focused on just why such delays happened – and why they were so much more dramatic among black than among white young adults in the latest generations. An important part of the delayed marriage trend resulted from increases in education. Chapter 4 showed striking increases in formal schooling for each new generation during the 1900s, with the Lucky Few men in particular making the biggest single leap forward. When we consider these educational trends separately for blacks and whites, the results help in understanding the tremendous recent delays in marriage for black Americans.

In simplest terms, each generation of black Americans just about matched the educational achievements of the *previous* generation of white Americans, but within this overall pattern, black generations gradually closed the gap with their white counterparts. Figure 8.6 illustrates this one-generation lag by presenting the educational distributions for white men and women in the Hard Timer, Good Warrior and Lucky Few generations, side-by-side with similar distributions for black men and women one generation younger – that is, Good Warriors, Lucky Few and Baby Boomers.

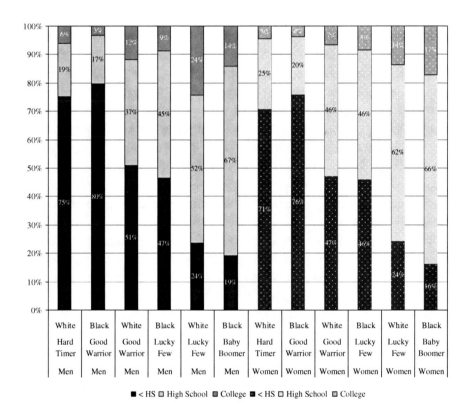

Fig. 8.6 Shrinking black–white lag in education
Source: Original calculations from Census Public Use Microdata Samples.

About three-fourths of the first generation shown in the figure for each race/sex group failed to complete high school – but this first generation involved white Hard Timers counted in 1940, compared to black Good Warriors counted in 1960. Even when lagged a whole generation, more blacks than whites failed to complete high school. Over time, however, successive new black generations made faster progress in completing high school than did white generations. Already by the second generation in each series, the share of black men and women in the Lucky Few failing to finish high school as of 1977 actually dropped below the share for white Good Warriors from 1960, one sign of the progress made by the Lucky Few in general. This faster progress in completing high school continued for the third generations shown in the figure, with particularly fast progress visible by 1996 for black Baby Boom women compared to white Lucky Few women in 1977.

While black women also lagged about a generation behind white women in receiving college diplomas, this college gap was even more serious for black men – they have lagged nearly two generations behind white men in graduating from college. There have been notable exceptions, of course. For example, important pioneers in the civil rights movement in mid-twentieth century America included black college graduates like Martin Luther King (Morehouse College in Atlanta), Jesse Jackson (North Carolina A&T University), James Meredith (University of Mississippi), Black Panther founder Huey Newton (Merritt College in Oakland, California), and Stokely Carmichael (Howard University in Washington DC) – all members of the Lucky Few.

Black Lucky Few college graduates also include sociologist William Julius Wilson (Wilberforce University in Ohio) and Harry Edwards (San Jose State University). Tennis star Arthur Ashe attended UCLA on a tennis scholarship before going on to become the only African-American man ever to win the Wimbledon, U.S. Open or Australian Open tennis tournaments. Humorist and writer Bill Cosby graduated from Temple University. Football star and actor Jim Brown, one of the greatest running backs of all time in his years with the Cleveland Browns, attended Syracuse University on a football scholarship after a local benefactor paid for his first year of college there. Taken together, though, black men in every generation remain under-represented among the ranks of college graduates.

The two-generation lag behind whites for black men finishing college, compared to the one-generation lag for black women, produced another distinctive educational result for black Americans, even though the black-white gap for both sexes did close gradually during the century. In every generation considered, black women surpassed black men in rates of college graduation – the opposite of the pattern for whites until Generation X extended this pattern to whites as well. Predominance of women among black college students remains particularly strong in professional schools (except schools of business, where women remain scarce no matter whether they are black or white). At the start of the twenty-first century, two-thirds of all black students enrolling in law school were women (Journal of Blacks in Higher Education 2000). Lucky Few member Jocelyn Elders (born Minnie Lee Jones in 1933 to poor sharecropper parents in Arkansas) picked cotton with her seven brothers and sisters as a child, but started on her path to becoming the first black female U.S. Surgeon General when she enrolled in a historically black school, Philander Smith College, at the age of 15. After a tour of duty in the Army, Elders benefited from the G.I. bill and completed the University of Arkansas Medical School, becoming one of the three first black students to earn an M.D. degree there and later earning a Master of Science in biochemistry.

Greater leaps forward in education for each successive generation of black Americans compared to whites, particularly among women, play an important part in explaining why the delayed marriage trend was more dramatic among blacks. As people stay in school longer they tend to marry at older ages, and educational gains have been stronger for black women than for any other group in American society over the course of the century. Education is not the entire story, however. We also must consider the changing career environments of successive generations.

Employment Patterns in Black and White

Reinforcing particularly strong effects of educational progress among black women from one generation to the next, differences in employment trends also help to explain why the most recent generations of black Americans delayed marriage so much more than did whites. Family formation always has depended on economic resources and success, no matter what one's race or sex or generation. We saw in Chapter 4 that rising levels of prosperity in American society during the early twentieth century played a major role in the gradual shift of marriages to younger ages. If we want to see why black Baby Boomers and Gen Xers delayed marriage so dramatically, we must consider employment patterns for men as well as for women.

The "normal" level of employment among black men in middle adulthood lagged behind the level for whites in both the Good Warrior and Lucky Few generations. For instance, in 1967 when the median Lucky Few men reached age 30 (see Fig. 8.7), about 88 percent of

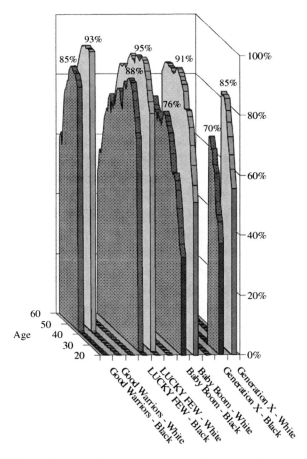

Fig. 8.7 Black–white employment contrast for men by generation (with peak rates)
Source: Original calculations from Census Public Use Microdata Samples.

the black Lucky Few men held paying jobs, compared to 95 percent of white Lucky Few men. These peak rates for the Lucky Few exceeded the peak rates observed among Hard Timers by a few percentage points, but in both generations, employment levels for black men lagged about seven or eight percentage points behind the rates for whites. The combination of a post-war economic boom and the small size of the Lucky Few generation drew black as well as white men into the work force in unprecedented numbers, providing the closest thing to full employment ever seen by any generation, particularly in young adulthood.

After the Lucky Few, though, the "normal" employment deficit of black compared to white men began to magnify. Not only did twice as big a share of young Baby Boomer men overall remain without jobs in the family-forming ages, but Fig. 8.7 also shows a wider black/white employment gap during the difficult early careers of Baby Boom men.

The mid-century economic boom eventually gave way to the oil crisis of the 1970s, supply-side economics, ballooning federal budget deficits that doubled the national debt in a decade, and a slowing economy that could not absorb the huge Baby Boom generation. Richard Easterlin (1980) discusses these trends in his book *Birth and Fortune* under the label of *stagflation* – stagnation of the economy amid rising unemployment rates, combined with high rates of price inflation. Peak employment rates were not observed for Baby Boom men until their median members reached age 35 in 1990, five years older than for the Lucky Few.

Though Baby Boom men generally had serious problems finding jobs, these problems were much more severe for blacks than for whites. Figure 8.7 shows peak employment rates of 91 per cent for white male Baby Boomers, but only 76 percent for black male Baby Boomers. The gap between peak rates for blacks and whites had doubled from seven or eight percentage points to fifteen. While we probably have not yet observed the peak employment rates for men in Generation X, Fig. 8.7 shows that the new 15-percentage-point gap has persisted in this generation as well as among the Baby Boomers. With black men in particular in the Baby Boom and Generation X having so much more trouble entering the work force, no one should be surprised to find that they delayed marriage dramatically.

At the same time, employment trends for women present an even more intriguing contrast in black and white. Among both the Lucky Few and the Good Warriors, black women actually were more likely to hold paying jobs than were white women. Figure 8.8 displays the higher peak rates observed for black women in these generations. Peak employment rates for black women in both generations refer to years when their median members were just under 50 years old, while the peak rates for white women in these generations refer to median ages of 52 in both cases. The earlier peak employment age for black than for white women among the Good Warriors and the Lucky Few probably reflects greater concentration of black women in blue-collar and service work, occupations where earnings peak earlier

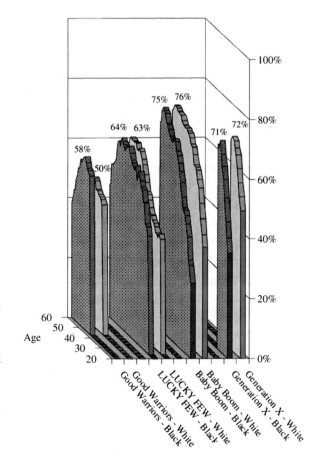

Fig. 8.8 Black–white employment contrast for women by generation (with peak rates)
Source: original calculations from Census Public Use Microdata Samples.

in life than in the pink-collar ghetto or professions like teaching and nursing.

The peak employment rates shown in Fig. 8.8 for women later in life only tell half the story, though. For example, almost identical peak rates for black and white women in the Lucky Few could lead to an initial impression of almost no difference in paid employment. A closer look at the figure shows that this impression would be very wrong. Employment rates for young black women rose much higher than for young white women in the Lucky Few, because many white women were staying at home at these ages to care for their Baby Boom babies, lagging behind the men in their generation in both educational attainment and labor force participation gains. This homemaking and childcare took a large "bite" out of the employment rates for white women at younger ages in Fig. 8.8, so that they also lagged far behind black women in paid work. For example, at median age 32 (that is, in 1969, twenty years before their peak employment rates) 42 percent of white Lucky Few women had paying jobs, while 55 percent of black Lucky Few women were employed. Black women did not have as much luxury of choice about staying at home with children. Even though black Lucky Few women did help contribute to the birth rate boom, black Lucky Few mothers remained in paying jobs more than whites.

Employment problems noted above for young black Baby Boomer men also appear among young black Baby Boomer women in Fig. 8.8. Rapid employment gains by white Baby Boomer women erased the black employment surplus found in earlier generations. Peak employment rates for Baby Boom women (at median age 45 in the year 2000) again give an initial impression of almost no difference between blacks and whites, but this time such an impression errs in the other direction. Among Boomers, for the first time white women had higher employment rates than black women at all ages. For example, at all median ages from 20 to 28 (that is, from 1975 to 1983) white Baby Boom women had paid employment rates that exceeded rates for black Baby Boom women by about twelve percentage points – the reverse of the gap observed among young women in the Lucky Few. Essentially the same employment deficit in early adulthood appears among black women compared to white women in Generation X.

How Lucky were Black Americans in the Lucky Few?

All in all, then, should we see membership in the Lucky Few as a matter of good fortune for black as well as for white Americans? The evidence for a positive answer seems very strong throughout the chapter above. Black men and women in the Lucky Few made faster progress (relative to earlier black generations) in both education and employment than did the white Lucky Few (relative to earlier white generations). The race gap in American society narrowed among the Lucky Few in many tangible ways. In other ways, however, black Lucky Few members grew up just a little too early to enjoy "lucky" changes still in their future. The desegregation of hospitals, public schools, mass transportation, hotels, restaurants, gas station bathrooms and the rest of everyday American life did not come in time for the Lucky Few, at least not in time for the innocent years of childhood or the exploratory ages of adolescence. As noted in Chapter 1, black members of the Lucky Few had the hard responsibility to act as civil rights pioneers, risking (and even sometimes losing) their lives and their livelihood in the struggle that would produce much better opportunities not just for a few but for many of their children and grandchildren in the Baby Boom, Generation X and the New Boomers. This chapter sketched some important ways in which black Americans shared in the good luck of the Lucky Few. But we must not forget that the youth and young adulthood of the Lucky Few did pass in an America where the distinction between black and white still retained much of its historic significance, and still exerted an important effect in its own right (for good or for ill) on the life chances of people living in the United States.

Note

1. Divisions are groups of states that combine to form the four Census Regions – West, South, Central (sometimes called Midwest) and Northeast. For example the South region includes the South Atlantic, East South Central and West South Central divisions. The Census Bureau website offers maps detailing all these boundaries.

Chapter 9
The Best Time to Retire

Contents

The Challenge of Intergenerational Transfers

Every society must come to terms with one basic fact in order to continue through history with its hard-won knowledge and material accomplishments – the fact that each of its members is "temporary." Each historical generation eventually gives way to the next as we are born, live and die. Infants and young children depend on the care and attention of the larger group. In old age, people again depend on the care and attention of the larger group. Every society must invent a reliable, systematic way to provide for this demographic metabolism, to transfer care and resources from productive adults to youthful and elderly dependents.

In centuries past, the family reigned supreme as the institution assuring such intergenerational transfers. Parents cared for (and had custody over) their children, and also managed to take care of the few elderly kin who survived into old age. The key to security and support, as the old saying had it, was to "pick your ancestors carefully."

During the twentieth century, elderly dependents took on new significance in the United States and other advanced countries. People reaching old age increased both in absolute numbers and as a share of the population. When this happened, the traditional familistic system for intergenerational transfers could no longer handle the job, and new societal arrangements had to be invented – inventions like government-organized Social Security, collecting resources from the entire population of economically active adults and transferring them to the growing population of aged dependents.

The Aged Dependency Ratio relates the number of people 65 years old or older to the number in the "working ages" from 15 to 64. The 1900 Census showed only six people at age 65 or over for every hundred people between ages 15 and 64, but by 2000 this ratio swelled to *twenty* people 65 or over for every hundred people 15–64. The ratio is rising even higher in the early twenty-first century as the first Baby Boomers reach retirement ages. It is no accident that Social Security was introduced as the share of elderly dependents increased.

What produced these dramatic shifts in the age distribution of the American population? Why did the share of older persons increase between 1900 and 2000? Improved survival provides part of the explanation for the growing number (and share) of older Americans in the population.

Survival of Generations

Like my father's elder brother (whose name I inherited) some people die as children – that is, before age 15 according to the conventional definition. Others manage to reach adult working ages, only to die before reaching retirement age. My own father worked all of his adult life but died from cancer at age 59, never collecting a penny of the Social Security or other pension benefits that he had earned. Finally, some people (most people today) survive through both childhood and the working ages, dying at some point after the conventional retirement age of 65.

We can find cross-sectional snapshots of survival conditions for any specific year in Statistical Abstracts of the United States, or from the

National Center for Health Statistics internet site (*http://www.cdc.gov /nchs/nvss.htm*). To examine generational patterns in survival, however, we must rearrange these annual age-specific statistics into cohort-oriented survival rates, following birth cohorts as they age through different years instead. Fortunately, demographers at the University of California at Berkeley already have re-arranged these age-specific rates to follow birth cohorts for the entire twentieth century in the United States.

Figure 9.1 uses cohort survival figures from the Berkeley Mortality Database (*http://www.demog.berkeley.edu/~bmd/*) to calculate what share of each generation died before age 15 ("childhood") and between ages 15 and 64 (the "working ages"). The balance of each generation, of course, died or will die at age 65 or older because in the end the death rate always remains the same – one to a customer.

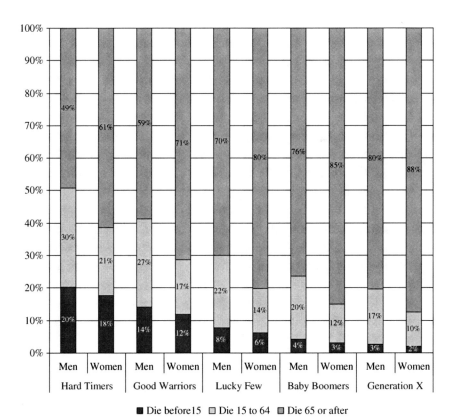

Fig. 9.1 Percent dying in selected age ranges
Source: Cohort survival rates from Berkeley Mortality Database.

Since New Worlders (born before the twentieth century) do not appear as cohorts in the Berkeley Mortality Database, we begin with the Hard Timer generation. New Boomers, born at the other end of the century, are too young to estimate most of their lifetime survival patterns, so we conclude with Generation X. Indeed, neither Baby Boomers nor Generation X have reached an average age of 65 yet. Their survival for ages they haven't yet reached is estimated in the database by applying projected mortality rates expected in the future to the members of these generations after their latest available ages.

This figure confirms an observation made in Chapter 2, that a full one-fifth of Hard Timer boys and almost one-fifth of Hard Timer girls died in childhood. Survival improved for each generation, particularly among children, so the percentage dying before their fifteenth birthdays dropped to single digits for the Lucky Few. Only about two percent of Generation X failed to reach age 15. Prevented deaths before age 15 don't make the population older, though. These survival improvements actually made the population younger at first, because so many extra children survived to be counted in the population.

Only half of all Hard Timer men actually made it from birth to age 65. Hard Timer women survived a bit better as adults, losing less than 40 percent of the entire generation before age 65. Although adult survival didn't increase as fast as improvements for children, a century of steady progress against mortality at all ages meant that the share in Generation X expected to die by age 65 (20 percent of men and 12 percent of women) should rival the share of the Hard Timers who died before age 15 (20 percent of men and 17 percent of women) – a tremendous improvement in survival. Instead of losing one-third to one-half of a generation before retirement, the newer generations realistically can expect that most people will reach retirement and live for many years thereafter. In fact, in recent decades death rates fell fastest at the oldest ages, and prevented deaths at these ages do make the population older, because these prevented deaths are above the average age of the population.

Falling Birth Rates and Population Aging

While better survival (particularly at older ages) has become important for the aging of the U.S. population, falling birth rates actually had a much bigger impact on the rising average age. Figure 4.6 in Chapter 4 above showed the sharp decline in the average number of children born to mothers in each succeeding generation, except for the temporary "blip" among the Lucky Few during the Baby Boom. Falling birth rates reduce the share of the population in younger generations. Continued falling birth rates for such new small generations compound the effect, shifting the average age of the population upward.

The Child Dependency Ratio (people younger than 15 divided by people in the working ages) fell during the century due to falling birth rates and smaller families, at the same time that the Aged Dependency Ratio (people 65 or over divided by people in the working ages) increased as noted above. The 1900 Census found 56 children under age 15 for every hundred people in the working ages, but by 2000 this ratio fell to only 32 children per hundred in the economically active ages. The total decline of 24 children per hundred working-age people easily outweighs the century-long increase of 14 more elderly people per hundred workers.

Measuring Trends in Dependency

Setting ages 15 and 65 as boundaries for what are usually called the working ages lets us choose benchmarks when we want to discuss improvements in survival. However, calling people under 15 or 65 and over "dependents" and referring to everyone between these ages as "economically active" distorts actual dependency patterns.

Not everyone beyond a 65th birthday should count as a dependent. New changes in Social Security regulations recently began to shift the normal retirement age of 65 toward older ages, so 65 will not remain the right boundary for anyone in the long run. Also, some people identify strongly with their jobs and remain active and healthy after age 65, so they don't want to retire. Laws preventing age discrimination have helped some of these men and women to keep working long after age 65. Other people without pension plans, family support or much life savings find it almost impossible to live on Social Security alone, so they have no choice but to keep working in what has been called the "pensioners' labor market" – for example, the well-known greeters in

Walmart stores, but also including waitresses, night watchmen, and other people who otherwise would be old enough to retire. They may have to wait a long time to become dependents, however much they might wish to do so.

In addition, not everyone at ages 15–64 should count as economically active either – if by that we mean earning money in the economy, paying taxes, and contributing to pension plans and other retirement programs (the source of transfer payments to dependents). Many young people stay in school long past age 15. Though some of them may combine part-time jobs with formal education, many still must be considered dependents in any strict economic sense of the term. Early in the century, most women between ages 15 and 64 worked at home without pay rather than in the paid labor force. Although farm wives might well have been enumerated in censuses as farmers along with their husbands, they were not. For other women, housework certainly counts as work but most housewives earned no wages, paid no taxes, and had no pensions except as survivors of their husbands. Thus they also should be thought of as dependents. Other adults at ages 15–64 find that various disabilities (discussed again below) force them out of the labor force prematurely, and make them dependents.

A significant fraction of workers retire early from their jobs, starting to collect Social Security benefits at age 62. Such early retirement also undermines the validity of age 65 as a boundary. As we saw in Chapter 4, more men in each generation leave the labor force while still in the supposedly economically active ages. People retiring "early" (that is, before normal retirement ages) may claim that they are not dependents – that they are supporting themselves with money they earned. They may not be claimed as dependents by any other particular individual(s) in the working-age population, but most of these early retirees do depend on employed people to keep the economy going, to keep their dividends and interest and rents and pensions and other forms of non-wage income flowing in to support them without their own participation in the labor force.

Accordingly, we consider not only people's ages but also whether they belong to the paid labor force. This seems essential when examining economic dependency in a society dominated by the money economy. In that economy, every person in the United States is either a dependent or a worker transferring resources to dependents.

Long-Term Improvement in the Dependency Ratio

Calculations for Fig. 9.2 divide the number of dependents outside the labor force by the number of workers in the labor force, to show the number of dependents per worker. Early entrants to the labor force (under age 15) and people working past normal retirement ages (over age 65) count in the bottom of this ratio as part of the labor force. At the same time, people in the "working ages" who don't actually belong to the paid labor force (students without paying jobs, home-makers, early retirees, working-age adults on disability pensions, and so on) appear in the top of our ratio as dependents. Figure 9.2 shows very dramatic long-term improvement in the balance between workers in the labor force and people who rely on them for support.

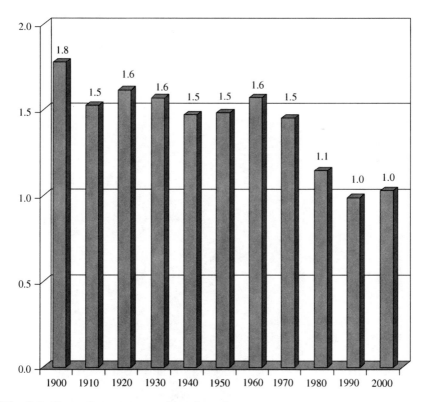

Fig. 9.2 Dependents per employed worker
Source: Original calculations from Census and CPS Public Use Microdata Samples.

In 1900 nearly two dependents relied on every worker in the labor force. That is, about one-third of the population supported the other two-thirds. However, with a short interruption due to more young dependents during the Baby Boom (see 1950–1970) this level of dependency dropped steadily – from nearly two dependents per worker at the start of the century to only one dependent per worker by the end of the century.

We further divide dependents into the three traditional age groups – under 15, 15–64, and 65 or over – that add up to the total of all dependents. (No age distinctions divide those in the labor force – they count all together as the denominator for all groups of dependents.) This way of dividing up all dependents, as illustrated in Fig. 9.3, shows the dramatic decline of dependents under age 15 caused by falling birth rates. It also demonstrates clearly that throughout the twentieth century a major and rapidly-changing share of dependents actually appeared within what people often call the "working ages." In fact, dependents within the working ages vastly outnumber dependents 65 or over throughout the whole century, right down to the present day.

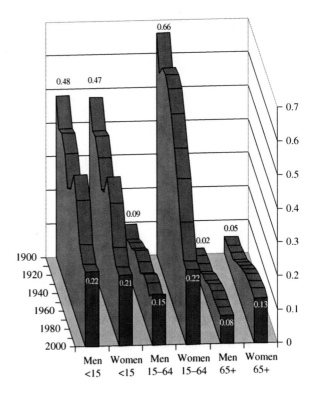

Fig. 9.3 Dependents per employed worker by age and sex Souce: Original calculations from Census and CPS Public Use Microdata Samples.

Women without paid employment account for most of the working-age dependents in the early decades of the century, and also experienced the biggest changes over time. Especially beginning after mid-century, women in the working ages began to take paying jobs alongside men. Whenever a person such as a housewife shifted from unpaid work to working in the paid labor force, she had a double impact on our ratio of dependents per worker – she disappeared from the ranks of dependents (reducing the numerator) and reappeared instead as a paid worker (enlarging the denominator). On the other hand, the trend toward longer school enrolments for dependent students in young adulthood and earlier retirement for men, both discussed in Chapter 4 above, changed numerator and denominator in just the opposite way, reducing workers and adding to dependents simultaneously.

The share of people 65 or older did increase, as also shown in the Figure. But fewer children in the population and the shift of working-age women into the labor force more than compensated for rising shares of older people, and produced the long-term decline in dependents per worker. These simple but rather overwhelming changes played an important role in the higher material living standards enjoyed by Americans in the final decades of the twentieth century, since the burden of transferring resources to dependents got lighter and could be shared among more workers.

The dependency ratio shown in Fig. 9.2 reached its minimum around 1990, though. It already has reversed and begun increasing again. Employment rates for women have nearly caught up with those of men in the youngest generations, and so cannot be expected to keep shooting upward in the future. Even though official retirement ages set by Social Security rules are rising slightly, the trend toward more people retiring earlier continues to gain momentum. Higher education shows no signs of withering away, and many students continue to rely on parental support. Though the shift from two dependents to only one dependent per worker has been very dramatic, this transition appears to be complete. The present pattern seems likely to remain for several decades into the future or even to be reversed as Baby Boomers retire.

The median member of the Lucky Few (born in 1937) began looking for a job just after mid-century, so the subsequent careers of this generation coincided with the decades when the United States cut the ratio of dependents to workers in half. Chapter 4 detailed near-universal employment of young Lucky Few men and rising rates of employment for women in the generation once their Baby Boom children had gone off to school. Chapter 6 revealed quantum leaps in occupational status for both men and women in the Lucky Few. As retirement ages approached, once again the Lucky Few found themselves in the right place at the right time. The first member of the Lucky Few (born in 1929) reached age 65 in 1994, squarely in the middle of the decade when the number of dependents per worker in the United States reached its historic low point. Throughout the following years, as the rest of the Lucky Few retired, the number of dependents per worker remained near this historic low level. Baby Boom workers at that point were in mid-career, paying huge amounts into pension funds and government accounts simply due to their numbers. Employment rates for women in the Baby Boom and in Generation X rose even higher than for the Lucky Few, further securing intergenerational transfers. The improved balance of workers per dependent guaranteed that the Lucky Few enjoy unprecedented levels of benefits in their old age.

Retirement Patterns for Generations

For a detailed look at generational changes in the gradual exit from paid employment, we capture a snapshot of each generation in the year when its median member reached the traditional retirement age of 65. This means we consider Hard Timers as they appeared in 1964 at ages 56–74, and Good Warriors some years later in 1983 at ages 55–74. We find the Lucky Few centered on age 65 as recently as 2002, when they occupied ages 57–73. In each of these years one of our generations reveals how its members experienced the transition from working life to retirement. The youngest members of each generation were mostly still working, even as the oldest members already were mostly retired. Figure 9.4 shows this transition for each of the three generations.

The most interesting and obvious difference in the retirement process for the Hard Timers, Good Warriors and Lucky Few appears in their late working lives as they pass age 55 and approach retirement. As noted in earlier chapters, successive generations of men began to retire earlier. Less than 10 percent of 57-year-old Hard Timer men had already left the labor force back in 1964. Only about 15 percent of 57-year-old Good Warrior men had given up paid employment as of

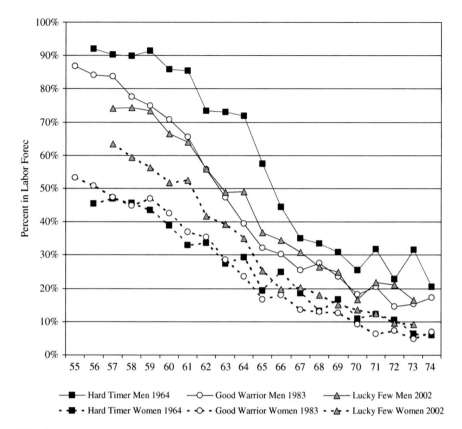

Fig. 9.4 Aging out of the labor force
Source: Original calculations from Current Population Survey Public Use
Microdata Samples.

1983. However, by 2002 more than 25 percent of the youngest Lucky
Few men at age 57 already had retired, long before the normal official
Social Security "finish line."

Such differences in the share of each generation retiring early fade
away with increasing age, though, as the generations converge on
conventional retirement ages. Older men in each generation shown
in Fig. 9.4 all had dropped to similar low levels of labor force participation (about one in five still working) by the time they reached
age 70.

On the other hand, the youngest Lucky Few women portrayed in
Fig. 9.4 (still in their late fifties) had more paying jobs in 2002 than
either Hard Timer or Good Warrior women at these ages in earlier

decades. These rising levels of employment for generations of women in their late fifties also fade away with increasing age, just as differences in early retirement faded away for men. Only one in ten among Hard Timer, Good Warrior, or Lucky Few women alike still had paying jobs at ages over 70.

Do these retirement trends single out the Lucky Few as more fortunate than earlier generations? Certainly earlier retirement for Lucky Few men seems to point to greater prosperity for them. On the other hand, to interpret higher employment rates for Lucky few women in their fifties as good luck, we would need to look at these paying jobs as signs of opportunity and fulfilment outside the home. Such a perspective contrasts sharply with the kind of good fortune attributed in Chapter 4 to Lucky Few women earlier in their lives, involving earlier marriages and more universal motherhood. Even within a single generation, then, good fortune may be viewed from different angles as the generation grows older, and may prove rather slippery to define.

Disability versus Active Life

Apart from government policies about Social Security eligibility and other age-related rules, many other factors figure in the decisions of people in every generation when they think about completing their careers. Some people may live part of their lives in good health, but may then spend an unfortunately long time suffering from various chronic ailments that multiply with increasing age (Nagi 1976). These issues of health and disability often play some role in retirement decisions.

In this connection we might look for trends involving various clinically-diagnosed disease conditions including hypertension, blindness perhaps resulting from glaucoma, high blood pressure, incontinence, depression, dementia, and other clinically diagnosed illnesses or injuries. Better statistics on such specific clinical conditions appear every day. However, precisely this rapid improvement in statistical information means that if we wish to look back over the course of the century, considering earlier generations as well as the present-day population, we rapidly run out of information. Little statistical evidence exists for clinical diagnoses in the population over the lifetimes of our earliest generations. Even today some clinical conditions may not be measured very well, so that systematic bias might exist in the extent to which we can identify these problems in different population groups.

A second alternative, therefore, considers the extent of specific kinds of health *outcomes* (rather than disease conditions) in the population. The most common measurements of health outcomes identify limitations in certain activities of daily living (or ADLs, as they are sometimes called). National statistics on ADL limitations record chronic problems with key areas of personal care: bathing or showering, dressing, getting in or out of bed or a chair, using the toilet, and eating. A person is considered to have an ADL limitation if any chronic condition(s) cause him or her to need regular, ongoing help with one or more of these specific activities (Wilder 1973).

The National Health Interview Survey (NHIS), conducted annually since 1957, includes a question about limitations that people experience with activities of daily living as just defined. NHIS results are available from the National Center for Health Statistics web site (see *http://www.cdc.gov/nchs/nhis.htm*) for years back to 1969. Figure 9.5 shows the responses to the NHIS question about ADL limitations for three of the generations covered here – the Hard Timers who reached ages 62–80 at the time of the 1970 NHIS, the Good Warriors who

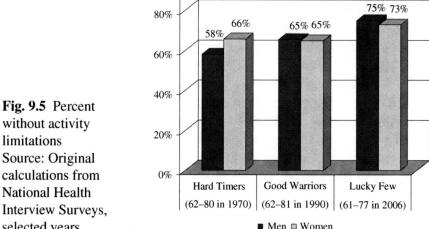

Fig. 9.5 Percent without activity limitations Source: Original calculations from National Health Interview Surveys, selected years.

were 62–81 years old when interviewed in 1990, and the Lucky Few reaching ages 61–77 in time for the 2006 NHIS.

When Hard Timers reached their sixties and seventies, women reported themselves in better health than men. Two-thirds of all Hard Timer women in 1970 said they had no physical limitations in their daily lives, while the equivalent share of men without such problems stood almost ten percentage points lower. Over time each new generation reported better health when they reached these early retirement ages (Crimmins & Satio 1997; Freedman et al, 2001). By 1990 when the Good Warriors reached these same ages, men in particular had reported encouraging progress in living free of any kind of limitation in their daily activities. The share of them reporting no limitations increased to match the two-thirds of women still reporting no problems with such activities.

This instance of men catching up to women's freedom from disabilities in the Good Warrior generation is one of the few examples of greater gains for men than for women in life conditions generally. Women's chances of actual survival increased faster than for men throughout most of the century. Women's gains in educational attainment exceeded men's in most generations (except for the Lucky Few). Women increased their employment faster than men in every decade and in every generation of the century, since they were playing "catch-up" to the men's earlier dominance of the paid labor force. Of course, we might point out that men have been leading the way in discretionary early retirement – what some might call "escape" from the labor force, and this might actually turn out to be related to their gains in disability-free life. Such a perspective remains unorthodox, though, in the United States where people regard work as a virtue and idleness as a vice, and where we work longer hours and more weeks in the year than almost any other developed country in the world.

The positive trend in disability-free living advanced even more for the Lucky Few. Once again men gained faster than women. By 2006, a full three-fourths of all Lucky Few men in their 60s and 70s reported no limitations in activity at all, higher than the 73 percent of Lucky Few women who could make the same claim. One important reason for the greater gains by men in avoiding disability probably involved the long-term shift from farm occupations (more common for New Worlders and Hard Timers) through blue-collar and craft occupations (in which the Good Warriors led the way) into white-collar and professional careers (the specialty of the Lucky Few). This dramatic shift in working conditions cut the chances for work-related injuries and the bodily wear and tear of jobs involving hard physical labor. Rising real income for each generation provided more chances for better health care as well, and the same preponderance of peacetime military service for the many Lucky Few veterans that kept their combat deaths to a minimum might also have contributed to their avoidance of disabilities in old age.

All in all, not only the quantity of life (years lived), but also the quality of life (freedom from limitations in the activities of daily living) improved in each new generation of Americans in the twentieth century. By 2026 the Baby Boomers will be in the same age range as shown for these earlier generations in Fig. 9.5. By then we will see whether the progress has continued for another generation. At the dawn of the new century, though, the Lucky Few rank as the healthiest generation so far in American history.

Trends in Marriage, Widowhood and Divorce

Earlier chapters already showed that successive American generations improved their economic situations. Each generation shifted into more prestigious and better-paying occupations than previous generations, with better working conditions and fewer hazards. Each generation took better advantage of more opportunities to invest in stocks, participate in pension plans, and in general improve their financial picture relative to earlier generations. The trend toward earlier retirement for men in successive generations offers one clear indicator of these improving economic circumstances.

This chapter has added improvements in survival and better health in old age (fewer limitations in the activities of daily living) to the picture of generational progress, at least for generations up through the Lucky Few who have reached older ages. How has all this progress affected home life for our generations as they grow older?

One way to look at everyday life for people reaching older ages considers the marriages they formed at an earlier life stage – those same marriages already described and discussed in Chapter 4. Figure 9.6 shows marital status distributions for four generations, comparing them when each had reached a median age of 70 (using

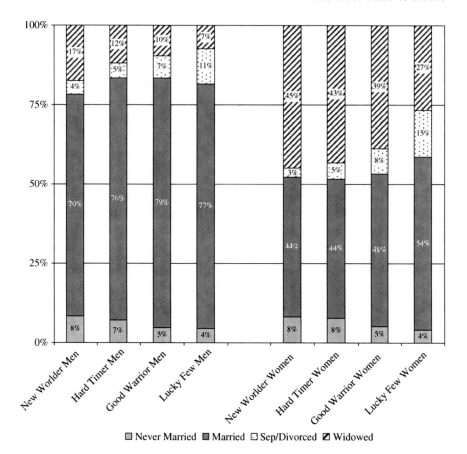

Fig. 9.6 Marital status by sex and generation at median age 70
Source: Original calculations from Census and CPS Public Use Microdata
Samples.

the 1950 Census for New Worlders, the 1970 Census for Hard Timers,
the 1990 Census for Good Warriors, and the 2007 Current Population Survey for the Lucky Few). Official Census marital status
categories considered here include never married (also called single),
married (all legally married couples, whether a spouse is present or
not), legally separated or divorced, and widowed. Unmarried cohabitation became an important consideration for our youngest generations, but such cohabitation played a much smaller role for earlier
generations in old age and retirement. For this reason, we examine
only the four long-standing categories listed above.

Progress for successive generations appears again in this figure, this time for marriage. At average age 70, each generation of women in particular included a larger share married than previous generations. The picture is not quite so clear for men. Hard Timer, Good Warrior and Lucky Few men all reported virtually identical percentages married at these ages.

One reason for the rising share of women married in each new generation can be found in steady contraction of the never-married group among both men and women – Chapter 4 also made this point earlier. But an even more important reason for more extensive marriage at older ages appears here as well – the dramatic decline in widowhood. This is to be expected, of course, given what already has been said in this chapter about improving survival, but the results for generations in old age still are striking. The share of widowers among men at median age 70 fell by more than half from the New Worlders to the Lucky Few (from 17 percent to 7 percent). While the equivalent share of widows among women did not fall by half, the absolute decline of 18 percentage points (from 45 percent of New Worlder women to 27 percent of Lucky Few women widowed) actually was much greater than the absolute decline for men.

The only sour note in this melody of more extensive marriage is sounded by the statistics for separation and divorce. In this respect the Lucky Few do not appear to be so lucky. The percentage of men reporting that they were divorced when their generations averaged 70 years old nearly tripled from 4 percent of New Worlders to 11 percent of the Lucky Few. For women the share separated or divorced increased even faster, from 3 percent to 15 percent for the same generations. This only counts the people still reporting themselves as divorced at each census or survey date, too; it does not include any formerly divorced people who have gotten married again. This is one important reason why fewer men than women report themselves as divorced even though every divorce produces one divorced man for each divorced woman–men remarry after divorce more frequently and faster than do women.

The Lucky Few eventually could still emerge as the luckiest generation of the century in terms of surviving marriages, because the share of marriages surviving into old age reflects two offsetting trends – a falling share of widows and widowers (due to better survival) and a rising share of divorced couples (due to rising divorce rates and less remarriage). Survival improved relatively fast for the first few generations of the century, and divorce rates increased slowly at first. This is why the Lucky Few surpassed earlier generations in surviving marriages.

Neither the survival trend nor divorce rates seem likely to continue on their earlier paths, however. Once widowhood falls to a low level, less room remains for improvement. On the other hand, the divorce rate continued to accelerate throughout the century. We simply cannot yet see the equivalent statistical results for Baby Boomers or Generation X, because Boomers will not reach an average age of 70 until the year 2035, and Generation X will not reach this point in life until 2061. Divorce trends in both these generations already are running well ahead of the Lucky Few. If rising divorce rates disrupt marriages faster than slowing survival improvements preserve them, the share married in old age for Baby Boomers or Generation X might fall below levels attained in old age by the Lucky Few. As with other speculations about these young generations, only time will tell on this score.

Trends in Independent Living

Living arrangements for people as they grow older provide another way to look at everyday life, a slightly different angle of vision from the discussion of marriage, divorce and widowhood above. Information about people's living arrangements comes from a Census and Current Population Survey question about "relationship to the household head."[1] In Chapter 3 this same question showed us some children in each generation living with grandparents or single parents rather than with both parents.

Figure 9.7 collapses many detailed categories of responses into four main groups, again comparing generations when each of them was centered on age 70. First, "independent, with spouse" means people who live independently in a married couple – that is, a couple where one partner is householder/head of household (see above footnote). A quick comparison reveals slightly higher percentages of men reported as "married" in Fig. 9.6 than as "independent, with spouse" in Fig. 9.7 Though the categories are similar, this is no mistake. This small discrepancy reflects the fact that a few married

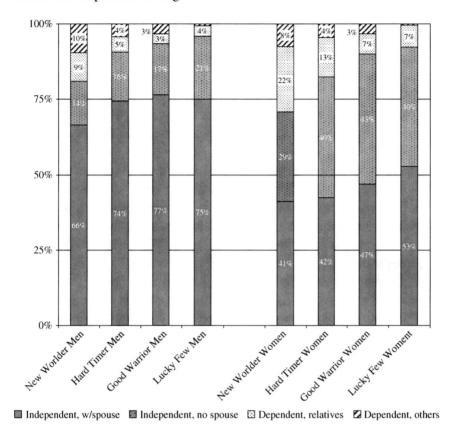

Independent, w/spouse ■ Independent, no spouse ▣ Dependent, relatives ▨ Dependent, others

Fig. 9.7 Living arrangements by sex and generation at median age 70
Source: Original calculations from Census and CPS Public Use Microdata
Samples.

couples at these advanced ages are no longer able to live independently. Both spouses live together as dependents in someone else's household.

Second, "independent, no spouse" means people who live independently without being married, including people who live alone, single parents heading a household with their dependent children, people living as an unmarried partner or housemate of a household head, and so on. Many more women than men fall into this second category.

Third, "dependent, relatives" means people who live in a household headed by a relative other than a spouse – most often an adult child of the respondent, or perhaps a sibling or some other relative. This arrangement, also more common for women than for men in old age, was much more prevalent at the beginning of the 1900s than it is today. It gradually diminished across the generations shown in the figure.

Fourth and finally, "dependents, other" means living as a dependent in some other kind of household headed by someone who is not a relative, such as living as a lodger or in group quarters – a very small category for most generations in the twentieth century, though it was still important for New Worlders in their old age as observed in 1950.

Men in every generation generally live independently even in old age, and have become more independent in each successive generation. Eighty percent of all New Worlder men lived independently when their generation reached a median age of 70 in 1950, and this percentage rose to fully 96 percent of Lucky Few men at equivalent ages after the turn of the century. The few older men living in someone else's household (when that someone else was not a spouse) were split between households headed by relatives (usually an adult child) and other situations, but the non-family settings virtually disappeared by the time we reach the Lucky Few.

Not only do older men live independently, but they usually do so as part of a married couple. The fact that many more women survive into these old ages than do men (see Fig. 9.1) means that any older man who comes to the end of a marriage (whether by divorce or widowhood) finds himself almost literally "surrounded" by unmarried women. In the generations studied here, up to and including the Lucky Few, traditional gender role specialization also left most of these men with only limited domestic skills, so to maintain independent living they often married again fairly quickly. Three-fourths of all older men among Hard Timers, Good Warriors and Lucky Few alike lived in independent married couples. Figure 9.7 also shows a gradual decline of dependence on relatives, and an increase in independent living even among unmarried men. This makes sense when we recall their improving financial situation, and particularly their improving health and avoidance of limitations in the activities of daily living.

The picture of progress in independent living is much the same for women at median age 70 in these same generations. Some important differences from men do leap out from Fig. 9.7, however. For one thing, although the share of women living independently comes quite close to the share for men in each generation overall, a much smaller share of these independent women remain married. Their smaller share married again reflects the greater numbers of women who survive to any particular age, and is further reduced because women generally are several years younger than their husbands – recall the gap between the average ages of mothers and fathers, shown in Fig. 3.4 for children in Chapter 3. Older husbands are more likely to have died, leaving their wives in the unmarried portion of the populations shown in Fig. 9.7.

Although it is true that the share of women living in independent marriages at these ages increased for each generation (from 41 percent of New Worlder women to a majority of 53 percent of Lucky Few women), the share of women living independently *without* marriages has increased just as fast, if not faster. The category that has declined the most, the mirror-image of these gains in independence, involves women who live as dependents in the homes of relatives. For example, my maternal grandmother (an immigrant New Worlder born in 1880) lived with her eldest daughter, my mother's older sister, to the end of her life. She was among the 22 percent of New Worlder women in that situation when their generation reached median age 70 in 1950. On the other hand, my own mother (born in 1911 and so part of the Good Warrior generation) has enjoyed better health, Social Security and Medicare benefits, and defined-benefit pension income from her years as a teacher. She still lives independently even though my father died more than three decades ago. She has never considered moving in with me or with my sister. She appeared among the 43 percent of Good Warrior women in Fig. 9.7 who lived independently but were no longer married by 1990.

Like my mother, many of these older women who no longer have husbands live alone (Macunovich et al, 1995), either in their former-family homes or in apartments after downsizing a household. Fran Kobrin (1976), one of the first scholars to examine the rapid increase in such living arrangements for older women, could have been talking about my mother when she attributed the tremendous increase in the number of older women living on their own to three separate factors:

1. faster increase in survival chances for women compared to men,
2. improvements in health status (examined above in terms of disability) that allowed them to remain active and independent, and

3. the spread of financial supports for independent living, including Social Security, Medicare, pensions from their own lifetime employment, survivors' benefit plans built up by their husbands, and other accumulated wealth such as real estate, stocks and bonds.

Lucky Few women enjoyed the greatest improvements in all three of these categories so far witnessed by any generation. Evidence in future decades may show Baby Boom and Generation X women achieving even greater self-reliance and independence, just as Richard Easterlin predicts in the introduction to this volume, but so far the Lucky Few look very fortunate.

Not all older women in the post-marriage stage of life lived alone, however. Although the share of them living as dependents with relatives fell dramatically, hundreds of thousands of these women contributed to the emergence of new kinds of living arrangements rarely seen at the beginning of the twentieth century. Sociologist Arlie Hochschild published *The Unexpected Community* in 1973, just as these new patterns of later-life living arrangements were coming to public attention. Her book documents the transformation of an old motel in Oakland, California into a residential community. The two-storey U-shaped structure has many counterparts all over the United States, places where travelers once stopped overnight but which eventually were swallowed up inside growing cities. The motel gradually became an apartment building specializing as a residence for older women living alone – and in the process, provided the physical setting for the emergence of new forms of social interaction, friendships, and even a surprising and unexpected sense of community among the women who lived there.

The award-winning television comedy *Golden Girls*, broadcast from 1985 to 1992, depicted something similar to the actual patterns studied by Hochschild. When Rose Nylund from the Midwest (played by Good Warrior actress Betty White) and Blanche Devereaux from the South (played by Lucky Few actress Rue McClanahan) found themselves alone after their marriages ended, they both moved into the Florida home of Dorothy Zbornak (Good Warrior actress Bea Arthur), a retiree from the urban east coast who already lived with her mother Sophia (Good Warrior actress Estelle Getty, actually younger than either Bea Arthur or Betty White). This "unexpected community" of non-relatives sharing a house, coming to terms with their ethnic and regional differences and the challenges of aging gracefully, faithfully reflected the innovative living arrangements being invented by older American women.

In the last quarter of the twentieth century, pioneering *ad hoc* communities like the residential motel studied by Hochschild or the shared house made famous by the *Golden Girls* have been joined by a vast, rapidly-expanding universe of new housing patterns including congregate housing, independent living complexes, assisted-living facilities, and countless other special structures and organizations, all created by entrepreneurs responding to the demands of increasing numbers of older Americans (particularly women) and to the increasing complexity of their everyday circumstances. In fact, it seems safe to say that we haven't yet seen the real growth spurt of this new industry at all – that is just beginning today, as the enormous Baby Boom generation finally reaches the ages where these new and complex living arrangements become a part of their world. Whether Baby Boomers as a whole will be lucky enough to measure up to the successes achieved by the Lucky Few in this regard remains (as always in this chapter) to be seen.

Our panorama drawn from the lifetimes of seven generations living through the twentieth century concludes with this look at retirement and later life. This chapter adds some additional records set by the Lucky Few, including record levels of survival into old age, record proportions of men and women living free of disabilities well into retirement, record levels of economic support, and resulting record levels of independence in later life for men and women, both for married couples and for people living on their own.

For all of these issues arising later in life, however, we run out of century before we run out of generations. We can't complete the story for Baby Boomers, Generation X, or the New Boomers. Any of these generations could turn out even luckier than the Lucky Few on some of these points. The next (and final) chapter shows one possible way to handle such incomplete trends, making an explicit comparison of the two generations of the century that were smaller (at least in early life) than the ones before them – the Lucky Few and Generation X.

Note

1. The term "head of household" was developed by the Census Bureau to organize data for all the people counted together in one residence or household – a dwelling unit with common kitchen and bathroom facilities, a common entrance, and so on. A household could occupy a farm house on the prairie, one apartment in a high-rise urban apartment building, a mobile home parked in a forest, or a variety of other living places. One person in each household was designated as the head, and each other person living there was classified in relation to that head of household – as the household head's spouse, son, daughter, parent, sibling, roommate, unmarried partner, and so on. Census enumerators traditionally had instructions to list the man in any married couple as the head of the household, and to list his wife as spouse of the household head. For this reason, men appearing in all Census and Current Population Survey data before 1980 are never listed as spouse of the household head. The term "head of household" disappeared from census forms in 1980, to be replaced by "householder." Also beginning in 1980, enumerators asked whose name appeared on house titles or rent contracts and listed that person first as the householder. If such information wasn't known, anyone could be listed as householder and normally the old practice of listing men first predominated.

   To deal with this historical peculiarity, we count married couples together as an independent couple if one or the other spouse was listed as householder or head of household – both husband and wife are counted as "independent," no matter whick one is officially listed as the head or householder. We count any unmarried person (including never-married, separated, divorced or widowed people) as "independent" if they are the head of the household where they live (including many older people who live alone as "single-person households"), or if they are living with an unmarried partner who heads the household (the unmarried equivalent of a married couple). If a person lives in a household where some other relative is listed as the head (for example, the respondent's brother or daughter or son-in-law) we count the person as a "dependent" living with relatives. If some other non-relative is listed as the head of a person's household, we count the person as a "dependent" living with other non-relatives, as shown in Fig. 9.6.

Chapter 10
Could It Happen Again?

Contents

Are the Few Always Fortunate?

The Lucky Few are not the only Americans forming a small generation as the twentieth century fades into a memory. Another one – Generation X – figured repeatedly in interesting comparisons with the Lucky Few in preceding chapters. About 66 million births in the United States between 1965 and 1982 left Generation X about ten million births short of the total for Baby Boomers born before 1965, and five million fewer than for New Boomers born after 1982. Though Generation X subsequently gained several million new members through renewed immigration, even in adulthood this generation remains smaller than the Baby Boomer and New Boomer generations on either side of them in history.

If the experiences of the Lucky Few furnish any guide to the future, a casual observer might conclude that the advantages of a less numerous generation should appear for Generation X just as they did for the Lucky Few born some forty years before them. Richard Easterlin touched on this issue in his book, *Birth and Fortune*, but at the time he was writing, Generation X had barely appeared on the scene and little or nothing was known about how life would turn out for them. He could only suggest (Easterlin 1987:146) that in general, "...a generation's fortunes have come to depend, as never before, on how numerous it is. If one is lucky enough to be born when the national birth rate is low – to come from a small generation – then one may look forward to a relatively bright future. If one has the misfortune of being a member of a large generation, then one's future is correspondingly dim." More specifically, referring to Generation X born after the Baby Boom (though not by name) he further observed, "As this small generation reaches adulthood, their fortunes will prosper like those of the young adults of the 1950s, and social and economic conditions generally should improve." (Easterlin: 1987:148)

At this writing the youngest members of Generation X already have celebrated a twenty-fifth birthday and the oldest among them are over age forty, so we can at least inspect the first decades of their lives. This chapter examines key aspects of the first half of the lifespan for the Lucky Few and for Generation X, including their living arrangements as children, their educational attainment, the timing of their decisions about marriage and childbearing, and their success (or lack of it) in the world of work and occupations.

Childhood for Small Generations

Generation X, as we saw in Chapter 3, had the youngest parents of any generation in the twentieth century. Their mothers and fathers, respectively, averaged about 26 and 29 years old when the Gen Xers were born. By comparison, the Lucky Few had older parents (average ages 28 and 33 respectively), so parents of the Lucky Few were more established in life when they became parents.

Recall, too, that Generation X had such youthful parents mainly because those parents usually had so few children. For most of the century, the Lucky Few were most likely to be "only children" compared to other generations. Generation X broke that record – one of every five of them were "only children," and over half of Generation X grew up either as an only child or with just one sibling in early childhood.

Extended beyond the immediate parental household, this pattern meant that Generation X children not only had few or no brothers and sisters, but also fewer cousins, and it meant that they were less likely than other generations to encounter other children of their own age in the neighborhood. In other words, their "peer networks" were more thin and sparse than for any earlier generation of Americans. Lucky Few children also lacked siblings and other playmates, but Generation X has taken the trend to new extremes.

For Generation X, parental supervision more often involved a single mother than for earlier generations. While only 4 percent of the Lucky Few were counted as living with only their mothers while under the age of ten, this increased to 6 percent of Baby Boomer children, and then doubled again to over 12 percent of Generation X children. As noted in Chapter 8, this share rose even higher for black children in Generation X – over 20 percent lived with single mothers, and only about half of all black Generation X children lived in a home headed by any kind of married couple.

We cannot link this rise of single mothers to generation size, however, because Baby Boomer children had more single mothers than the Lucky Few, and New Boomer children also had more single mothers than Generation X. This general weakening of the family as an intimate care-giving institution has not resulted primarily from generation sizes.

The point is that Generation X children were much less lucky than Lucky Few children in terms of childhood home environments. Fewer fathers at home, fewer brothers and sisters, fewer cousins and neighbor children, more and younger single mothers, all combined to produce a bleaker picture for Generation X as they took their first tentative steps in life. None of these changes suggest that Generation X was "lucky" in any sense of the word.

Small Generations in School

As already shown in Fig. 3.6 in Chapter 3, these disadvantages in early home life did *not* carry over into disadvantages in schooling for Generation X, when comparing them to the Lucky Few. Although the Lucky Few outdid the Good Warriors and other earlier generations in formal schooling, this good luck mainly applied to Lucky Few men.

It is hard to attach the label "lucky" to Lucky Few women in terms of education. They were the only generation of women who dropped out of high school as often as men, and they lagged far behind Lucky Few men in attending college. In fact, the gender gap in higher education actually opened widest for the Lucky Few (see Chapter 3).

In contrast, both Baby Boomer and Generation X women as well as men continued to set new records in educational attainment – another trend (like more fragile families for children) unrelated to generation size. Formal schooling became more nearly universal and complete in each new generation. By the end of the century, sixteen or more years of formal schooling had become a normal part of growing up in the American middle class – something that only a tiny handful of New Worlders ever attained back in 1900. Women in Generation X not only set new records for schooling compared to earlier generations of women, but actually graduated from college more often than men in their generation for the first time in American history.

Jobs for Small Generations

Figures 4.1 and 4.2 in Chapter 4 compared employment rates for generations centered on the ages of their median members, as each generation found its way into the paid labor force. Comparing the Lucky Few and Generation X in these figures yields very simple and straightforward conclusions.

First, men in both generations began entering the labor force at almost identical rates. When each generation's median members reached age 21 (in 1962 for the Lucky Few and in 1999 for Generation X) almost identical proportions (about 77 or 78 percent) of men in each generation had found jobs. However, Generation X men quickly dropped behind the rate of employment achieved by Lucky Few men over subsequent ages we are able to compare. By the time the median member of each generation reached age 29 (the oldest available median age for Generation X), the Lucky Few had rocketed upward to 92 percent of all men employed (still three percentage points short of their eventual peak at 95 percent). Generation X only managed to increase to 82 percent of men with jobs at the same ages.

In fact, this 82 percent figure reached by Generation X at median age 29 is identical to the sorry economic performance of Baby

Boomer men. The men in Generation X seem to be following in the shallower economic footsteps of male Baby Boomers, rather than following the record-breaking paths of Lucky Few men. Being part of a small generation has not made the men of Generation X "lucky" when it comes to jobs. Many reasons might account for this lack of good fortune, including millions of young Generation X immigrants who have cancelled out some of this generation's smaller size, differences in macro-economic conditions that this new small generation has faced, a possible "hangover" effect of Baby Boom men still competing with Generation X for jobs (as noted by Easterlin in the Introduction above), and even perhaps more direct competition with more of the young women in their generation, who are now participating fully in the job market. Whatever the explanation, one thing is clear: in terms of jobs, Lucky Few men were very lucky but Generation X men were not.

For women, on the other hand, we might even reverse the characterization just given for men above. Each new generation of women has taken paying jobs earlier and in greater numbers than the generation before them, and Generation X has been no exception to this rule. Generation X women made unprecedented progress into management and professional positions. By comparison, Lucky Few women postponed work and careers, staying home with Baby Boom babies instead. When they did go to work later in their lives, jobs for Lucky Few women usually concentrated in the pink-collar ghetto, unlike the progress of many Lucky Few men into corporate management and professions. In terms of jobs, then, Generation X women have been considerably luckier than Lucky Few women.

A pattern seems to be emerging here – in both schooling and jobs, the Lucky Few was above all a lucky generation for *men*, and perhaps not so much so for women. By comparison, *women* in Generation X have made more progress in both schooling and jobs than men. In Generation X the educational attainment, work lives and employment rates of men and women have become more alike than ever before. If Generation X became the first American generation with a larger share of women than men graduating from college, perhaps the New Boomers eventually could show us an even more striking picture – a generation with a larger share of women than men employed! A few more decades will be needed to judge such a question.

Marriage and Childbearing in Small Generations

More than any other indicator of their good fortune in life, the early
marriage trend and the era of "motherhood mania" championed by the
Lucky Few seem to exemplify their optimism and the opportunities
that blossomed on every side for the century's first smaller generation. Here it is enough to recall (see Chapter 4) that for the Lucky
Few, the age at marriage dropped to the lowest level on record in
American history, proportions ever marrying reached historic highs,
and the share becoming parents also exceeded the share for any other
studied generation.

How does Generation X compare on these points? Again the answer is clear and straightforward. Figure 4.3 in Chapter 4 already
has shown us that both men and women in Generation X have been
more reluctant about getting married than any previous generation of
the entire century. Not only have they fallen away from the record-
breaking early marriage trend of the Lucky Few, but they have set
new records for avoiding marriage. Figure 8.4 in Chapter 8 illustrated
the dramatic fact that over half of all black men and women in Generation X still had never married by 2003, when the median members of this generation already had reached age 29. The figures are
only a little less dramatic among whites. Young adults in our newest
generations continue to form intimate relationships, but today these
often lead to unmarried cohabitation rather than marriage (Clarkberg
et al 1995, Manning & Landale 1996, Bumpass & Lu 2000). For Generation X, living in married couples has become just one of many
specialized lifestyles, rather than occupying center stage as "the" normal way of life. Of course, Generation X also is staying in school
longer and in greater numbers than did earlier generations, so some
of this apparent scarcity of marriages may eventually be caught up at
older ages. Still, the fact remains that Generation X will spend much
less of its life married than did earlier generations, particularly the
Lucky Few.

Similarly, the era of "motherhood mania" has given way to renewed
higher proportions of childless women. The big difference here is that
before the Lucky Few, higher childlessness among New Worlders,
Hard Timers and Good Warriors usually was involuntary (Poston &
Gotard 1977). People without marriage partners generally avoided
parenthood, and social pressures that enforced these norms for the

unmarried might qualify such childlessness as involuntary. Couples without children usually suffered from some kind of reproductive impairments, and were widely pitied by those around them. Childless marriages had much higher rates of divorce than marriages with children. Today, by contrast, much of the resurgence of childlessness for Baby Boomers and Generation X has been voluntary and even deliberate (Jacobsen & Heaton 1991, Gillespie 2003). Today voluntarily childless marriages are actually more stable than marriages with children, although involuntary childlessness continues to destabilize marriages (Carlson 1982). Some childlessness for Generation X may be temporary, related to more schooling and later marriage. We know that although birth rates remain low for young women, birth rates among women in their thirties actually have been increasing in recent decades. No one expects such delayed births to fully make up the comparative scarcity of children for Generation X, however.

Do these contrasts in marriage and parenthood mean that Generation X has not been as lucky as the Lucky Few in this respect? Interpretation of such results is bound to be controversial. Traditionalists might point to young Generation X men having problems establishing careers, as well as Generation X women being "forced" by material circumstances to work, in explaining why Generation X have failed to match the marriage boom and early childbearing of the Lucky Few. On the other hand, progressives may see in this avoidance of marriage and childbearing the triumph of individualism, the pursuit of careers and self-actualization by both men and women, and so forth. Whatever the interpretation, it is certainly clear that if both men and women in Generation X are enjoying success and self-fulfilment, these outcomes are less often expressed by forming marriages and having children. Though luck may be in the eye of the beholder, something certainly has changed.

Attitudes of Small Generations

If the Lucky Few mark themselves by their answers on public opinion surveys as the most politically polarized generation of the century, Generation X appears to point the way back toward a more moderate, centrist pattern of public opinion. First of all, it is noteworthy that Generation X apparently has regained some of the confidence in major social institutions (see Fig. 7.2 in Chapter 7) that had been lost in earlier successive generations. They express more confidence in government, in big business (corporations) and in the military establishment (the Army) than did the Baby Boomers who came before them.

Republican political strategists might welcome the fact that Generation X members more often declare themselves to be Republicans than was true among the Baby Boomers. In fact, Generation X men report themselves as more Republican than Good Warriors or the Lucky Few, as well. Generation X women are about as Republican as the Lucky Few.

However, this may not turn out to be quite the news these strategists had hoped for, when we look a little deeper into the matter. It is true that Generation X has reversed the ebb tide away from the Republican party, even as they continue to abandon the Democratic party. However, narrow and noisy partisan elites with their professional pollsters, image spinners and personality assassins who dominate both parties provide an awkward fit with the new Generation X Republicans. The share of conservatives among Generation X Republicans falls even lower than the figure for Baby Boomer Republicans – only 51 percent of Generation X Republicans say they are "conservatives," compared to 60 percent of Lucky Few Republicans (see Fig. 7.10 in Chapter 7). In fact, one-third describe themselves as "moderates" and over 16 percent of Generation X Republicans describe themselves as "liberal," compared to only 11 percent for the polarized Lucky Few Republicans.

Democrats, on the other hand, simply have lost even more of their grasp on this latest generation. The share of Generation X identifying with the Democratic party dropped lower than for any other generation of the twentieth century. In fact, among men this decline was so steep (from 36 percent of Lucky Few men to only 24 percent of men in Generation X) that Generation X became the first generation in which Republican men actually outnumbered Democratic men in absolute terms. This was never the case in any previous generation of men.

Together, these two trends for Republicans and Democrats meant that the share of people skipping party identification altogether and claiming to be independents captures more of Generation X than any generation before them. Nearly half the people in Generation X (45 percent of men and 42 percent of women) refuse to identify with either political party, while less than a third (32 percent of men and 30 percent of women) called themselves independents among the

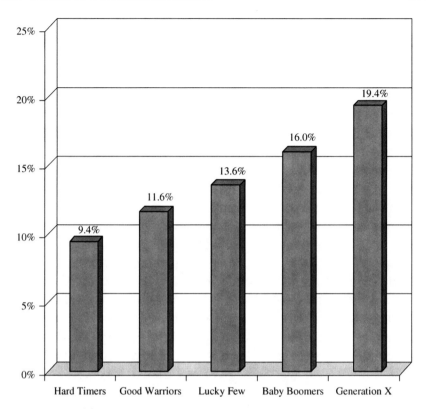

Fig. 10.1 Moderate independents by generation
Source: Original calculations from General Social Survey data.

Lucky Few. Among these self-declared independents, the share claiming to be liberal or conservative also has dropped. More than ever before, moderate independents are the biggest single political category in Generation X, outnumbering both "liberal democrats" and "conservative republicans" as shown in Fig. 10.1. (This also was true for Baby Boomers, but is even more the case in Generation X.)

The Context of Generational Fortunes

In some ways Generation X already has surpassed the Lucky Few. In other ways they never will. If Generation X, despite its small size, has not turned out to be "lucky" in quite the same way as the Lucky Few, what really does determine the fortunes of a generation? Certainly generation size contributes to the verdict, but the smaller size of these two generations must take its place as only one of many formative factors.

The renewed faith of Generation X in basic institutions including business, labor and government stands as a tribute to the strength and collective spirit of this generation. Their continuation of the trend toward greater political moderation bodes well for the future. They show every sign of setting new records for longevity and good health. All in all, members of Generation X already have begun to demonstrate their capacity to advance into adult roles and responsibilities as business and political leaders, as the parents of the New Boomers and future generations, and as taxpayers, voters, and citizens.

However, growing up in a relatively small generation did not save Generation X children from steady weakening of the family as an intimate care-giving institution, after the high-water mark achieved for Lucky Few children. Living in small generations did not stem the rising tide of divorce among adults for either the Lucky Few at mid-century or Generation X at the end of the century. The continued weak employment record of men in Generation X, following in the shallow footsteps of the Baby Boomers despite a decline in generation size, contrasts with the unprecedented success of Lucky Few men in their early careers and early retirements. On the other hand, Lucky Few women did not look so lucky when it came to education and jobs, while Generation X women have broken historic records for both schooling and employment.

These seeming inconsistencies highlight the importance of the social and economic landscape over which generations of any size must travel during their lives. Dramatic changes in fundamental social values concerning what kinds of gender roles are "good" (or even "normal") for men and for women have altered these social landscapes from one generation to the next, so that large or small generation size plays out as a disadvantage or an advantage in very different ways in different generations.

On their own terms, then, including their own generation-specific definitions of what it really means to be "lucky," the Lucky Few presented in this book will continue in some respects to reign as the most fortunate generation of Americans in the twentieth century. The really remarkable thing about the Lucky Few is that they, and their lifelong good fortune, have gone nearly unnoticed until now.

"As I look back, if I used one word I would use the word 'luck'. I just feel very lucky. Neil Armstrong was born in 1930. Buzz Aldrin was born in 1930. Mike Collins was born in 1930. How lucky can you get? We just happened along at the right time". (Apollo 11 Command Module Pilot Mike Collins, quoted from the motion picture *In the Shadow of the Moon.*)

References

Angrist, Joshua & Krueger, Alan. 1994. Why do World War II veterans earn more than nonveterans? *Journal of Labor Economics* 12(1): 74–97.

Auletta, Ken. 2005. *Media Man: Ted Turner's Improbable Empire*. New York: W. W. Norton.

Bengston, Verne. 1975. Generation and family effects in value socialization. *American Sociological Review* 40: 358–371.

Billingsley, Keith R. & Tucker, Clyde. 1987. Generations, status and party identification: a theory of operant conditioning. *Political Behavior* 9(4): 305–322.

Blake, Judith. 1989. *Family Size and Achievement*. Berkeley: University of California Press.

Bloom, David E. & Freeman, Richard B. 1992. The Fall in Private Pension Coverage in the United States. *American Economic Review* 82(2): 539–545.

Bly, Nellie. 1890. Around the World in Seventy-Two Days. New York: The Pictorial Weeklies Company.

Brodkin, Karen. 2000. *How Jews Became White Folks and What that Says About Race in America*. New Brunswick NJ: Rutgers University Press.

Brokaw, Tom. 1998. *The Greatest Generation*. New York: Random House.

Bumpass, Larry & Lu, Hsien-Hen. 2000. Trends in cohabitation and implications for children's family contexts in the United States. *Population Studies* 54: 29–41.

Carlson, Elwood. 1982. Dispersion of childbearing outside marriage. *Sociology and Social Research* 66(3): 335–347.

Carlson, Elwood. 1982. Motherhood and marital stability. *Social Forces* 61: 258–267.

Carlsson, Gosta & Karlsson, Katharina. 1970. Age, cohorts, and the generation of generations. *American Sociological Review* 35: 710–718.

Clarkberg, Marin; Stolzenberg, Ross; & Waite, Linda. 1995. Attitudes, values, and entrance into cohabitational versus marital unions. *Social Forces* 74: 609–632.

Converse, Philip E. 1976. *The Dynamics of Party Support: Cohort-Analyzing Party Identification*. Beverly Hills: Sage.

Crimmins, Eileen M. & Saito, Yasuhiko. 1997. Dominique Ingegneri Trends in disability-free life expectancy in the United States, 1970–90. *Population and Development Review* 23(3): 555–572

Cutler, Neal E. 1968. *The Alternative Effects of Generations and Aging Upon Political Behavior*. Oak Ridge TN: Oak Ridge National Laboratory, Study ORNL-4321.

Cutler, Neal. E. 1976. Generational approaches to political socialization. *Youth and Society* 8: 175–206.

Davis, Kingsley. 1940. The sociology of parent-youth conflict. *American Sociological Review* 5: 523–535.

Dawson, Deborah A.; Meny, J. Denise & Jeanne Clare, Ridley. 1980. Fertility control in the US before the contraceptive revolution. *Family Planning Perspectives*. 12(2): 76–86.

DeMartini, Joseph R. 1985. Change agents and generational relationships: a reevaluation of Mannheim's problem of generations. *Social Forces* 64(1): 1–16.

DeTray, Dennis. 1982. Veteran status as a screening device. *American Economic Review* 72(1): 133–142.

DuBois, W.E.B. 1940. *Dusk of Dawn: An Essay Toward an Autobiography of a Race Concept*. New York: Harcourt, Brace & Company.

Dunn, William. 1993. *The Baby Bust: A Generation Comes of Age*. Ithaca NY: American Demographics Books.

Easterlin, Richard A. 1961. The American baby boom in historical perspective. *The American Economic Review* 51(5): 869–911.

Easterlin, Richard A. 1966. Economic-demographic interactions and long swings in economic growth. *The American Economic Review* 56(5): 1063–1104.

Easterlin, Richard A. 1980. *Birth and Fortune: the Impact of Numbers on Personal Welfare*. Chicago: University of Chicago Press.

Eisenstadt, Smuel Noah. 1956. *From Generation to Generation: Age Groups and Social Structure*. Glencoe IL: Free Press.

Elder, Glen Jr. 1968. *Children of the Great Depression*. New York: Houghton Mifflin.

Eschbach, Karl; Supple, Khalil & Snipp, C. Matthew. 1998. Changes in racial identification and the educational attainment of American Indians, 1970–1990. *Demography* 35: 35–43.

Evan, William M. 1959. Cohort analysis of survey data: a procedure for studying long-term opinion change. *Public Opinion Quarterly* 23(1): 63–72.

Falbo, Toni. 1992. Social norms and the one-child family: clinical and policy implications. in F. Boer and J. Dunn (eds.). *Children's Sibling Relationships: Developmental and Clinical Issues*. Hillsdale, NJ: Lawrence Erlbaum.

Flacks, Richard 1967. The liberated generation: an exploration of the roots of student protest. *Journal of Social Issues* 23: 52–75.

Folger, John K. & Nam, B. Charles. 1967. *Education of the American Population: a 1960 Census Monograph*. Washington DC, U.S. Government Printing Office.

Foner, Nancy & Fredrickson, George (eds.). 2004. *Not Just Black and White*. New York: Russell Sage Foundation.

Freedman, Vicki A.; Crimmins, Eileen; Schoeni, F. Robert; Spillman, C. Brenda; Aykan, Hakan; Kramarow, Ellen; Land, Kenneth; Lubitz, James; Manton, Kenneth; Martin, G. Linda; Shinberg, Diane; Waidmann, Timothy. 2004. Resolving inconsistencies in trends in old-age disability: Report from a technical working group. *Demography* 41(3): 417–441.

Gibson, Campbell. 1976. The U.S. fertility decline, 1961–1975: the contribution of changes in marital status and marital fertility. *Family Planning Perspectives* 8(5): 249–252.

Gillespie, Rosemary. 2003. Childfree and feminine: understanding the gender identity of voluntarily childless women. *Gender and Society* 17: 122–136.

Glenn, Norval & Grimes, Michael. 1968. Aging, voting, and political interest. *American Sociological Review* 33: 563–575.

Glenn, Norval. 1973. Sources of the shifts to political independence: some evidence from a cohort analysis. *Social Science Quarterly* 53: 494–515.

Gregory, James. 2005. *The Southern Diaspora: How the Great Migrations of Black and White Southerners Transformed America*. Chapel Hill: UNC Press.

Grossman, James. 1989. *Land of Hope: Chicago, Black Southerners and the Great Migration*. Chicago: University of Chicago Press.

Gusfield, Joseph R. 1957. The problem of generations in an organizational structure. *Social Forces* 35: 325–330.

Hernandez, Donald J. 1993. *America's Children: Resources from Family, Government and the Economy*. New York: Russell Sage Foundation.

Hochschild, Arlie. 1973. *The Unexpected Community*. Englewood Cliffs, NJ: Prentice-Hall.

Howe, Neil & Strauss, William. 2000. *Millenials Rising*. New York: Random House.

Ignatiev, Noel. 1995. *How the Irish Became White*. London: Routledge.

Jacobson, Cardell & Heaton, Timothy. 1991. Voluntary childlessness among American men and women in the late 1980s. *Social Biology* 38: 79–73.

Journal of Blacks in Higher Education. 2000. Black women now dominate African-American law school enrollments. *JBHE* 64–66.

Kertzer, David I. 1983. Generation as a sociological problem. in R. Turner & J.F. Short (eds.). *Annual Review of Sociology*. Annual Reviews Inc.

Kilpatrick, Andrew. 2001. *Of Permanent Value: The Story of Warren Buffett*. New York: McGraw-Hill.

Klecka, William R. 1971. Applying political generations to the study of political behavior: A cohort analysis. *Public Opinion Quarterly* 35(3): 358–373.

Kobrin, Frances E. 1976. The fall in household size and the rise of the primary individual in the United States. *Demography* 13(1): 127–138.

Lancaster, Lynne & Stillman, David. 2002. *When Generations Collide*. New York: HarperCollins Publishers.

Laslett, Peter. 1972. *Household and Family in Past Time*. Cambridge: Cambridge University Press.

Le Bon, Gustave. 1894. *Les Lois psychologiques de l'évolution des peuples*. Paris: Ancienne Librairie Germer Bailliere.

Lewis, Gregory B. & Meesung Ha. 1988. Impact of the baby boom on career success in federal civil service. *Public Administration Review* 48(6): 951–956.

Lewis, Oscar. 1966. *La Vida*. New York: Random House.

Liebow, Elliot. 1967. *Tally's Corner*. Boston: Little, Brown and Company.

Lovejoy, Owen R. 1911. Seven years of child labor reform. *Annals of the American Academy of Political and Social Science*, 38 (Supplement: Uniform Child Labor Laws): 31–38.

Macunovich, Diane J.; Easterlin, A. Richard; Schaeffer, M. Christine; Crimmins, M. Eileen. 1995. Echoes of the Baby Boom and Bust: recent and prospective changes in living alone among elderly widows in the United States. *Demography* 32(1): 17–28.

Mannheim, Karl. 1923. Das Problem Der Generationen. *Koelner Viertelsjahresheft fuer Soziologie* 7: 157–180, 309–330.

Mannheim, Karl. 1927. The problem of generations. in K. Mannheim. *Essays on the Sociology of Knowledge*. London: Routledge & Kegan Paul.

Manning, Wendy & Landale, Nancy. 1996. Racial and ethnic differences in the role of cohabitation in premarital childbearing. *Journal of Marriage and the Family* 58: 63–77.

Martindale, Melanie & Poston, Dudley. 1979. Variations in veteran/non-veteran earnings patterns among World War II, Korea, and Vietnam war cohorts. *Armed Forces and Society* 5(2): 219–243.

Micklethwait, John & Wooldridge, Adrian. *The Company: A Short History of a Revolutionary Idea.* Wabash, St. Louis & Pacific Railroad Company v. Illinois, 118 *U.S.* 557 (1886).

Montagu, Ashley (ed.). 1964. *The Concept of Race.* New York: Collier.

Morgan, S. Philip. 1991. Late nineteenth- and early twentieth-century childlessness. *American Journal of Sociology* 97: 779–807.

Morrison, Peter. 1999. Family policies and demographic realities. in James Hughes & Joseph Seneca (eds.). *America's Demographic Tapestry: Baseline for the New Millenium.* Brunswick NJ: Rutgers University Press, pp. 34–39.

Nagi, Saad Z. 1976. An epidemiology of disability among adults in the United States. *The Milbank Memorial Fund Quarterly. Health and Society* 54(4): 439–467.

Nam, Charles B. 1964. Impact of the GI Bills on the educational level of the male population. *Social Forces* 43(1): 26–32.

Office of Management and Budget. 1977a. *Race and ethnic standards for Federal statistics and administrative reporting.* Washington DC: U.S. Government Printing Office.

Office of Management and Budget. 1997b. *Revisions to the standards for the classification of Federal data on race and ethnicity.* Federal Register 62FR58781-58790.

Omi, Michael & H. Winant. 1994. *Racial Formation in the United States: from the 1960s to the 1990s.* (2nd edition) New York: Routledge (see especially Chapter 4).

Oppenheimer, Valerie Kinkaid. 1967. The interaction of demand and supply and its effect on the female labor force in the U.S. *Population Studies* 21: 239–259.

Oppenheimer, Valerie Kincaid. 1970. *The Female Labor Force in the United States: Demographic and Economic Factors Governing Its Growth and Composition.* Berkeley: Institute of International Studies, University of California.

Oppenheimer, Valerie Kincaid. 1982. *Work and the Family: A Study in Social Demography.* New York: Academic Press.

Ortega y Gasset, Jose. 1923. *El tema de nuestra tiempo.* Madrid.

Ortega y Gasset, Jose. 1951. Die Idee Der Generationen. *Das Wesen geschichtlicher Krisen.* Stuttgart.

Ortega y Gasset, Jose. 1958. *Man and Crisis* (translated by Mildred Adams). New York: Norton.

Poston, Dudley & Erin Gotard. 1977. Trends in childlessness in the United States, 1910–1975. *Social Biology* 24: 213–224.

Poterba, James M.; Samwick, Andrew A.; Shleifer, Andrei & Shiller, Robert J. 1995. Stock ownership patterns, stock market fluctuations, and consumption. *Brookings Papers on Economic Activity* 2: 295–372.

Preston, Samuel. 1984. Diverging paths for America's dependents. *Demography* 21(4): 435–457.

Putnam, Robert. 2000. *Bowling Alone: the Collapse and Revival of American Community*. New York: Simon & Schuster.

Report of the President's Commision on an All-Volunteer Armed Force. 1970. Washington: U.S. Government Printing Office.

Richardson, John G. 1980. Variation in date of enactment of compulsory school attendance laws: an empirical inquiry. *Sociology of Education* 53(3): 153–163.

Rindfuss, Ronald. 1991. The young adult years: diversity, structural change, and fertility. *Demography* 28(4): 493–512.

Rintala, Marvin. 1963. A generation in politics: a definition. *Review of Politics* 25: 509–522.

Ryder, Norman. 1965. The cohort as a concept in the study of social change. *American Sociological Review* 30(6): 843–861.

Salerno, Salvatore & Guglielmo, Jennifer. 2003. *Are Italians White? How Race in Made in America*. London: Routledge.

Segal, David R. & Segal, Wechsler Mady. 2004. *America's Military Population*. Population Bulletin 59(4). Washington DC: Population Reference Bureau.

Skrabanek, Robert L. 1995. *We're Czechs*. San Antonio: Texas A&M University Press.

Smedley, Audrey. 1999. "Race" and the construction of human identity. *American Anthropologist* 100: 690–702.

Smith, James P. & Welch, Finis. 1981. No time to be young: the economic prospects for large cohorts in the United States. *Population and Development Review* 7(1): 71–83.

Strauss, William & Howe, Neil. 1991. *Generations: The History of America's Future, 1584 to 2069*. New York: William Morrow & Company.

Thomas, Eugene 1974. Generational discontinuity in beliefs: an exploration of the generation gap. *Journal of Social Issues* 30: 1–22.

Turner, Fredrick Jackson. 1893. The Significance of the Frontier in American History. Paper presented to the American Historical Association in Chicago.

U.S. Bureau of the Census. 1975. *Historical Census of the United States, Colonial Times to 1970, Becentennial Edition*. Washington DC: U.S. Governtment Printing Office.

Uhlenberg, Peter. 1974. Cohort variations in family life cycle experiences of U. S. females. *Journal of Marriage and the Family* 36(2): 284–292.

Vere, James. 2007. Fertility, female labor supply, and the new life choices of Generation X. *Demography* 44: 821–828.

Walters, Pamela & Briggs, M. Carl. 1993. The family economy, child labor and schooling: evidence from the early-twentieth-century South. *American Sociological Review* 58: 163–181.

Welch, Jack & Byrne, A. John. 2001. *Jack: Straight from the Gut*. New York: Warner Business Books.

Wilder, Charles S. 1973. U.S. National Center for Health Statistics. *Vital and Health Statistics Series 10, No. 80. Limitation of Activity Due to Chronic Conditions: United States, 1969 and 1970*. Washington DC: U.S. Government Printing Office.

Index

Printed in the United States
123065LV00002B/16/P